HOW IT WORKS

In Industry

ALLAN PUBLISHERS, INC.

Copyright © 1982, 1980 Walt Disney Productions
Published by Ottenheimer Publishers, Inc.
Exclusively distributed by Allan Publishers, Inc.
Baltimore, Maryland 21208
Printed in Great Britain.
All Rights Reserved.

WORKS
In Industry

Contents

offset lithography, gravure printing, newspaper production, linotype caster, color printing, automatic wrapping machine, shrink wrapping machine

Introduction

We live today in a world which is dominated by machines. Machines transport us and make most of the things we wear and use in the home, at work and at play. They also entertain us, process and package our food, and can even carry us into space. We live in what is often called "the Machine Age," but it was not always like this.

Until about 250 years ago there were only a handful of machines around, and these were worked by hand, by animals or by wind and flowing water. Then the steam engine was developed, which was able to provide mechanical power when and where it was wanted. Men began to build machines powered by steam. They employed workers to operate them and built factories to house them. People flocked from the countryside to work in the factories.

A revolution had begun – an Industrial Revolution. The revolution started in Britain. It started first in the

textile industry, but it soon spread to other countries and to other industries, particularly iron and steel, mining and transportation.

Today another industrial revolution is upon us. It is being brought about by what is called automation. Automation refers to the widespread use of automatic and self-adjusting machines, which require few or no human operators. In an automated factory the machines and processes are controlled not by man, but by another machine – a computer. We shall see more and more automation in the future because computers can now be made very small. They can be built into tiny crystal wafers made of silicon – called silicon "chips," or microprocessors.

Computers work much faster than human workers, and they can do many things at the same time, which human workers cannot. Also, they never tire, nor do they ask for raises!

7

Except in a few places in the world, the weather is not warm enough or dry enough all the year round for us to go around naked. We need to wear clothes to keep warm and dry. Clothes were one of the first things man made over 10 thousand years ago. Before that he wrapped himself in animal skins to keep warm.

Dyeing

Dye vat

Shuttle

Woof thread

Textiles

Rope-making

Hand spinning

Spindle

Whorl

Hand loom

Warp thread

Fabric

Spinning a Yarn

Cotton and wool are two of the most common materials used to make cloth. Cotton comes from the seed boll (pod) of cotton plants; wool from the fleece of sheep. Their fibers are quite short, a few centimeters long at the most, so they have to be joined and twisted together to make a continuous thread, or yarn, before they can be made into cloth. The process of spinning does this.

On a small scale, spinning can be done with the aid of a spinning wheel, but in industry a great many machines are employed, as the picture shows. The diagrams show the stages cotton goes through when it is spun.

The cotton arrives at the spinning mill tightly packed in hugh bales, which first have to be opened and broken up. This is done in the bale breaker and the opener, which also remove some of the dirt and twigs in the bales. The cotton is further separated and cleaned in the picker and beater, from which it emerges as a loose blanket, or lap.

The lap is then fed to a carding machine, where it is combed by rotating wire-toothed rollers. The carded cotton is gathered into loose ropes called sliver, which then go to the drawing, or drafting frame. On the frame several slivers are gathered together and

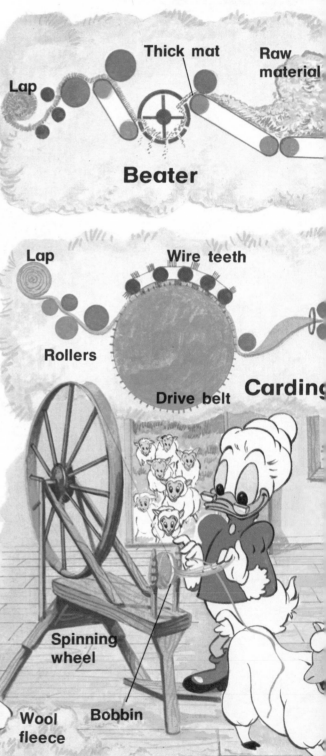

Raw fibers

Thick mat
Raw material
Lap
Beater

Lap
Wire teeth
Rollers
Drive belt
Carding

Spinning wheel

Wool fleece

Bobbin

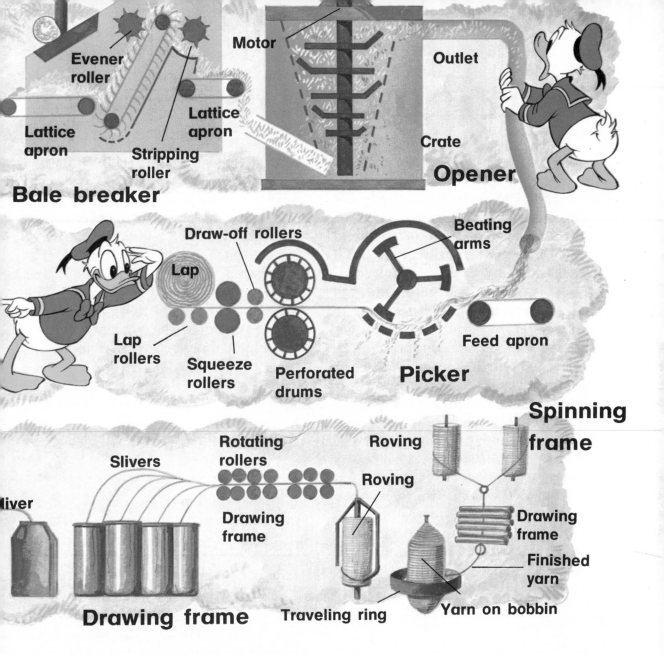

Bale breaker

Evener roller

Lattice apron

Lattice apron

Stripping roller

Motor

Outlet

Crate

Opener

Draw-off rollers

Lap

Lap rollers

Squeeze rollers

Perforated drums

Beating arms

Feed apron

Picker

Spinning frame

Roving

Slivers

Rotating rollers

Roving

Sliver

Drawing frame

Drawing frame

Finished yarn

Drawing frame

Traveling ring

Yarn on bobbin

passed through sets of rollers, each set rotating at increasing speed. The fibers are drawn out into a loose thread called roving.

The roving is now ready for final spinning on the ring spinning frame. It goes through more drafting rollers before being twisted and wound on a bobbin by a traveling ring.

Another widely used natural fiber comes from the stalk of the flax plant. It is spun into the yarn we call linen.

Silk comes from the cocoons "spun" by silkworms. It consists of very long threads hundreds of meters long. To make silk yarn, several threads are combined and lightly twisted, in a process known as throwing.

Weaving Cloth

Most of the fabrics we use are made by weaving. One set of threads is woven under and over another set of threads at right angles to it. In the simplest kind of weaving pattern, or weave, a thread crosses under and over the other threads alternately. This forms a pattern called plain weave. Sheets and handkerchiefs have a plain weave. In other weaves, one thread crosses under and over two or more threads.

Weaving is carried out on a machine called a loom. The factory loom works on the same principles as the hand loom, but it operates very much faster. The parts of a simple loom are shown in the small illustration. One set of yarns, the warp, is threaded lengthwise through the loom. The yarn passes through eyelets in wires (heddles), which are held in a frame (harness). There are two sets of heddles mounted in two harnesses. In operation one moves up as the other moves down.

When the heddles move in this way, a gap is opened between the two sets of warp yarns passing through them. This is called the shed, and it is through the shed that the crosswise yarn is passed to make a line of weave. The crosswise, or weft yarn, is carried by a shuttle. As soon as the shuttle has passed, a wire frame called the reed is pressed against the previous line of weave. Then the harnesses are reversed to make another shed; the shuttle is passed through it to make another line of weave; and the reed presses it against the previous line. These three processes, known as shedding, picking and

beating continue until all the warp yarn is used up.

There are various mechanical arrangements for shooting the shuttle through the shed to make a line of weave. One method of weft transfer is illustrated in the middle box. Some modern looms have no shuttle. The weft yarn is carried through the shed by kinds of needles ("rapiers"), by jets of air or water; or by other means.

Yarn **Harness** **Reed**

On the Carpet

Quite simple looms can be used to produce plain-weave cloth for handkerchiefs, sheets and the like, but if you want to produce a complicated weave, you need a more complicated loom which can separate different combinations of warp yarns when making a shed. The kind of loom used is called a Jacquard after the Frenchman who invented it nearly 200 years ago.

On a Jacquard loom the heddles that carry the warp yarns (page 13) are linked to a mechanism which can lift each one independently. The mechanism is worked by a series of punched cards, which contain details of the desired pattern in the arrangement of punched holes. Each line on the punched card represents a line of weave, and each hole in that line shows that a particular warp yarn has to be lifted. A needle-like sensing device finds out where the holes are and triggers a mechanism that lifts the appropriate heddles.

Jacquard looms are widely used to make carpets. Carpet weaving is rather different from ordinary fabric weaving. The warp and weft threads are interwoven as usual but around a backing material, which gives the carpet a firm foundation. Extra yarn is inserted in the weaving process to form the surface of the carpet, or pile.

Two well-known carpet weaves are called Wilton and Axminster, after the towns in Britain where they were first produced. In a Wilton carpet the pile is formed from loops of an extra warp yarn. The loops are cut to give ends to form a pile. In an Axminster carpet, however, the tufts of pile are inserted separately during weaving. A cheaper form of carpet called tufted carpet is made by looping yarn through a woven backing material. The tops of the loops are then cut off to produce a pile.

Wool used to be the favorite material for carpet pile, but it is now usually used in mixtures with man-made fibers (page 18) such as nylon and acrylic. The backing material is often jute or man-made fiber.

Jacquard mechanism

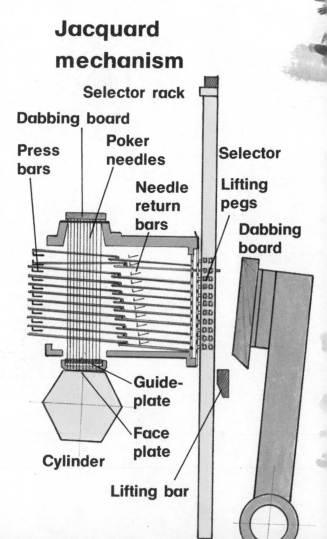

Selector rack

Dabbing board

Press bars

Poker needles

Needle return bars

Selector

Lifting pegs

Dabbing board

Guide-plate

Face plate

Cylinder

Lifting bar

Axminster weave

Warp yarns

Backing

Weft

Pile

Backing

Dyeing and Printing

The fibers used for making yarn are usually white, or slightly off-white in color, but we can produce colored fabrics by dyeing. Either the yarn can be dyed before weaving, or the fabric can be dyed after weaving.

Most fabric is dyed after weaving; but before dyeing can begin, the woven fabric must be thoroughly cleaned and bleached. Bleaching removes any natural coloring from the yarn and prepares it to receive the dye. In the bleaching process such chemicals as sulphur dioxide and sodium hypochlorite are used.

Most of the dyes used to color fabrics are man-made from chemicals. Different dyes have to be used for different fabrics. They come in many brilliant shades of all colors of the rainbow. They do not fade easily, so we say they are light-fast. The usual method of dyeing is to pass the cloth through a vat of hot dye solution.

Plain fabrics can also be colored by printing. A special kind of printing ink, or paste containing dye is applied to the fabric by rollers or silk screens. A design of different colors is produced by applying different colors one after the other.

In roller printing each color is printed by a roller which has the design engraved in it. The roller rotates in a trough of printing paste and is scraped by a knife blade, which removes the excess paste, leaving only the design itself covered with paste. It then rolls against the fabric, to which

the paste is transferred.

In silk-screen printing a piece of silk or similar fabric is treated with a gum or paint so that it only lets the printing paste through the design areas. The

Screen printing

Ink reservoir

Cloth

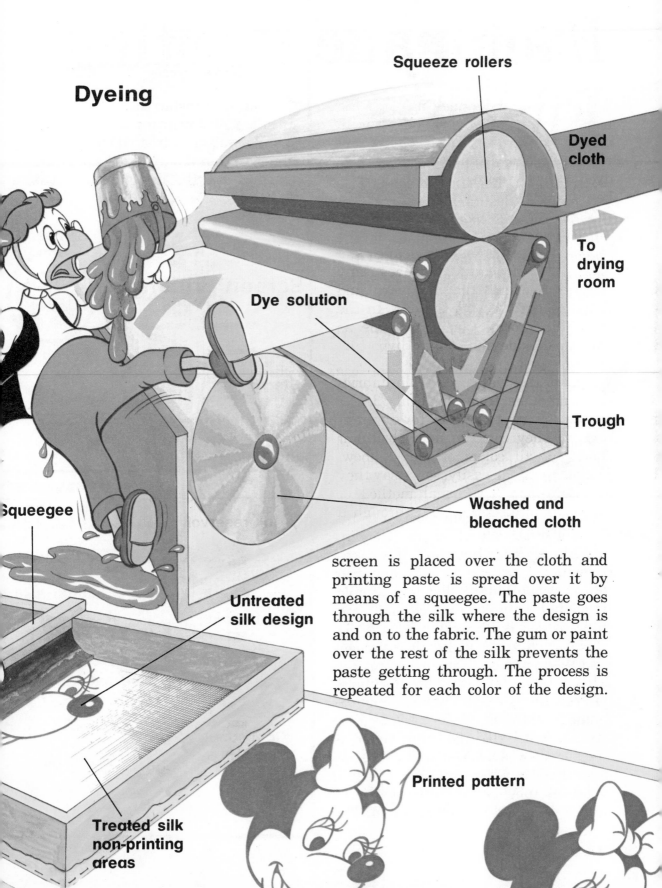

Dyeing

Squeeze rollers

Dyed cloth

To drying room

Dye solution

Trough

Squeegee

Washed and bleached cloth

Untreated silk design

screen is placed over the cloth and printing paste is spread over it by means of a squeegee. The paste goes through the silk where the design is and on to the fabric. The gum or paint over the rest of the silk prevents the paste getting through. The process is repeated for each color of the design.

Treated silk non-printing areas

Printed pattern

Man-made Fibers

Fibers such as cotton and wool have been used for thousands of years. They are found in Nature. Many of the fibers we use these days are made by man. One very common man-made fiber is rayon. It is made from woodpulp. Other man-made fibers, including nylon, orlon, polyester and acrilan, are made from chemicals manufactured in chemical plants. We call these synthetic fibers.

Most natural fibers occur in the form of short, or staple fibers, but man-made fibers are produced in the form of long, continuous threads, or filaments. These filaments can, however, be chopped up into staple fibers if required, and the staple fibers can be spun into yarn.

There are several ways of producing man-made fibers from plastics, woodpulp or other raw materials. They are usually termed "spinning" processes, though they are quite different from ordinary spinning. Nylon, for example, is made by a process called melt spinning, which is illustrated here.

Nylon chips are melted in a furnace and then pumped through a spinneret. This is a metal disc with fine holes pierced in it. As the molten nylon is pumped through, it forms into long strands which cool and become solid as they meet a stream of cold air. They may then be treated, or conditioned, in a steam tube before being gathered into a yarn and wound on a reel. The

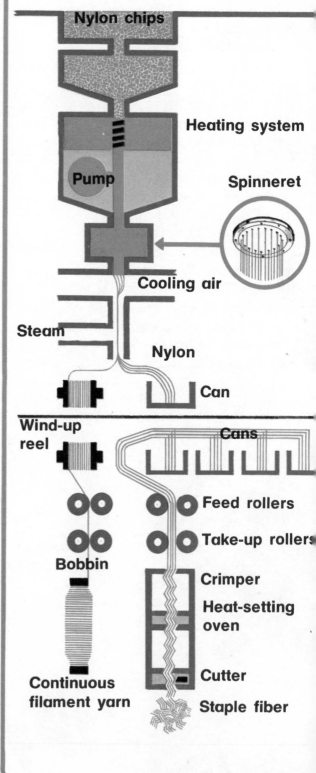

Nylon spinning

Nylon chips

Heating system

Pump

Spinneret

Cooling air

Steam

Nylon

Can

Wind-up reel

Cans

Feed rollers

Take-up rollers

Bobbin

Crimper

Heat-setting oven

Cutter

Continuous filament yarn

Staple fiber

yarn is then drawn out (stretched) by rotating rollers and wound on to a bobbin. Some of the nylon fibers may be chopped up into stable fibers.

There are several types of rayon made from woodpulp. They include viscose (the most common), acetate and triacetate. Viscose rayon is pure cellulose, the main substance in wood. Acetate and triacetate are chemicals made out of cellulose.

The small illustration outlines how acetate is made. Woodpulp is treated with chemicals and forms a solution of triacetate. After treating with other chemicals in a so-called ripening process, and adding water, flakes of acetate are formed. In the spinning process the flakes are dissolved and pumped through a spinneret. The fine streams of solution that emerge dry and form solid filaments.

Acetate rayon

Woodpulp — Oil

Chemicals

Catalyst — Cellulose triacetate — Solvent

Ripening, water added to form flakes

Flakes dried — Flakes washed

Storage — Acetic acid

Dissolving — Solvent

Solvent recovery — Filtration

Spinning — Staple fibers

Filament yarn

Knitting yarn

Gowns

Spacesuits

Children's clothes

Sportswear

Camping equipment

Metals

It would be difficult to imagine life without metals, for practically everything we use, eat or wear either contains metal, or has been made or handled by machines made of metal. The human race did not really begin to advance until it discovered how to make and use metals.

At first men used the metals they could find around them on and in the ground. Then they discovered how to make different metals from minerals.

They made first bronze and then iron. Bronze is a mixture of the metals copper and tin. It is what we call an alloy. We use most metals today in the form of mixtures, or alloys.

21

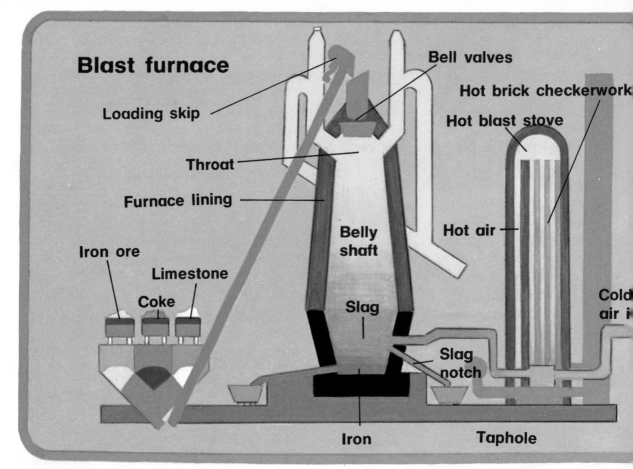

Blast furnace

Loading skip

Bell valves

Hot brick checkerwork

Hot blast stove

Throat

Furnace lining

Iron ore

Limestone

Coke

Belly shaft

Hot air

Slag

Hot blast stove

Cold air i

Slag notch

Iron

Taphole

Making Iron

The most important of all the metals we use is iron. We use iron most in the form of an alloy, which we call steel. The world uses something like 700 million tons of steel every year for making all manner of things, from nails and knives, car bodies and railroad lines, to skyscrapers and suspension bridges.

Iron is not found in the ground as a metal. It is found in the form of a chemical compound in minerals, or ores. It can be extracted from its ores

by heating them fiercely in a furnace. This process is called smelting.

Iron ore is smelted in a blast furnace, so called because a blast of hot air is blown in to make its fuel burn fiercely. The fuel in a blast furnace is coke. The coke also acts chemically to free the iron from the chemicals it is combined with in the ore.

In operation, the coke and iron ore, together with some limestone, are charged into the top of the blast furnace through double "bell" valves. The coke burns fiercely and also attacks the ore, freeing the iron. At the high temperature of the furnace (over 1,000°C) the iron is molten and falls to the bottom. A lot of the unwanted earthy matter in the ore combines with the added limestone to form what is called a slag. The slag also collects at the bottom of the furnace, floating on top of the molten iron.

From time to time the blast furnace is "tapped," or emptied. The slag and iron are removed separately. These days, the molten iron is often poured straight into huge ladles which take it for further processing. Sometimes it is poured into open molds called pigs, from which it gets its name – pig iron.

Many other metals are smelted from their ores, though the method of smelting may vary a great deal. Sometimes chemical methods are used to extract metals from their ores. Some copper ores are treated with acid to make them into a solution. Then the copper is recovered from the solution by passing electricity through it, in a process called electrolysis.

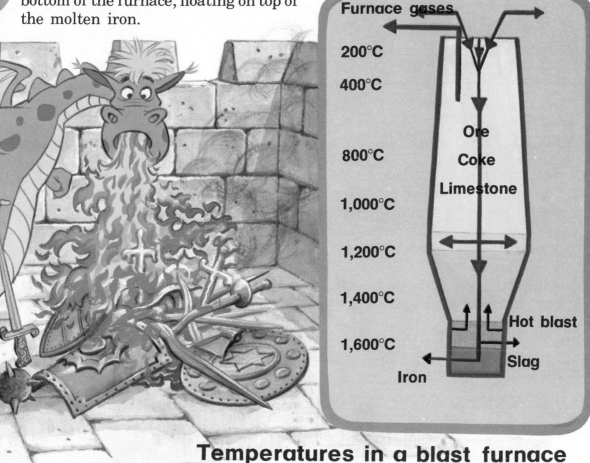

Temperatures in a blast furnace

Making Steel

The pig iron produced in the blast furnace (page 23) still contains much unwanted matter, particularly carbon (from the coke). These impurities have to be removed before the metal can be widely used. This process is called refining, and the metal that results is steel. Steel is an alloy, or mixture of iron with traces of carbon and other metals.

Refining also takes place in furnaces. The most important steel-making furnaces today are the basic-oxygen (BO) furnace and the electric-arc furnace. The BO furnace, or converter, is a huge steel cylinder lined, as all furnaces are, with fire-resistant brick (refractory). It is tilted for filling and emptying. It is filled with molten pig iron from the blast furnace, together with steel scrap.

Then a pipe, or lance, is lowered to the surface of the metal and oxygen is pumped through it at high speed. The oxygen is forced into the molten metal and burns out most of the impurities in an eruption of flames, sparks and smoke. After this so-called "blow," the metal has become steel.

In the electric-arc furnace steel scrap

Ladle

Molten steel

24

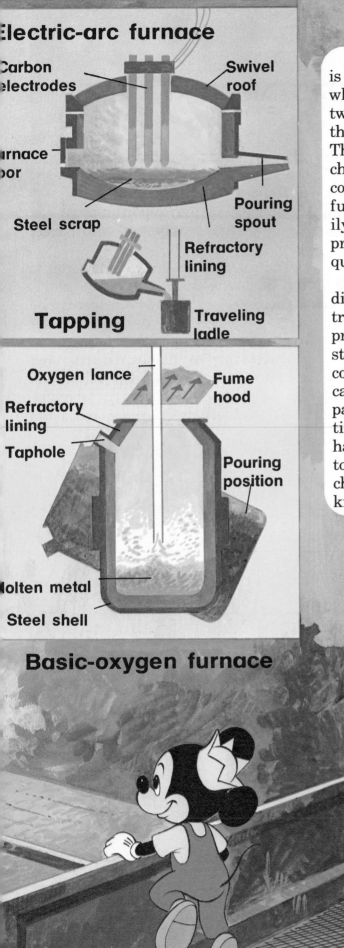

Electric-arc furnace

Carbon electrodes

Swivel roof

Furnace door

Steel scrap

Pouring spout

Refractory lining

Tapping

Traveling ladle

Oxygen lance

Fume hood

Refractory lining

Taphole

Pouring position

Molten metal

Steel shell

Basic-oxygen furnace

is generally used. The scrap is heated when electricity arcs, or jumps, between thick carbon rods (electrodes) in the roof, and the floor of the furnace. The type of steel scrap used is carefully chosen to produce steel of the right composition. Refining in an electric furnace is much cleaner and more easily controlled than in other furnaces. It produces steel of very much better quality.

The term "steel" is used for many different alloys of iron containing traces of carbon and other metals. The properties of these various kinds of steel depend on exactly what they contain. For example, ordinary steel, called mild steel, contains less than 1 part in 400 of carbon. Steel with six times as much carbon is very much harder and is used to make cutting tools and drill bits. Steel with lots of chromium and nickel does not rust; we know it as stainless steel.

Control room

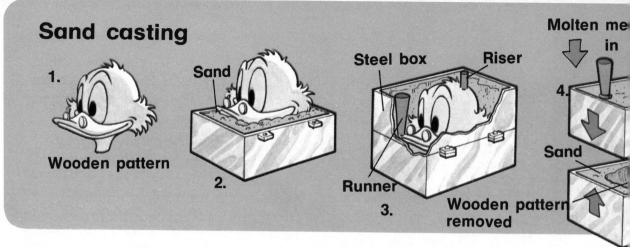

Sand casting

1.

Wooden pattern

Sand

2.

Steel box   **Riser**

Runner

3.

Molten me
in

4.

Sand

Wooden pattern
removed

Sand Casting

After the metal has been made in the furnaces, it is usually run into hollow cases, or molds, where it can cool. The solid metal blocks that form are known as ingots. The ingots then have to be turned into the form in which they will be used by one or more of a variety of shaping processes.

Sometimes the ingots are simply remelted and then poured into shaped molds. They take the shape of the molds when they cool. This method of shaping is called casting. The iron engine blocks of cars, for example, are made by casting.

The most common method of casting is sand casting, which is outlined in the numbered pictures. First a wooden pattern is made of the object you want to cast (1). Then the pattern is placed in the lower half of a steel box and a special kind of sand is packed firmly around it (2). Sand is then packed firmly around the upper part of the pattern in the other half of the box (3). Two wooden plugs (runner and riser) are put in the sand, touching the pattern. Next, the two halves of the box are separated, and the pattern is

26

5

Finished casting

removed. The two halves are put back together, leaving a hollow where the pattern was. The riser and runner plugs are removed (4).

Molten metal is then poured into the runner channel and flows into the hollow in the sand. The air inside escapes through the riser as the metal rises. When the metal has cooled, the two halves of the steel box are separated, and the rough casting (5) is removed from the sand. The casting is then smoothed and trimmed as need be, producing a fine object.

Rolling and Forging

Most metals are shaped not when molten (as in casting) but when solid. They are usually rolled, forged, pressed or machined (page 30). In rolling, the metal ingot is first heated until it is red hot and then it is passed time and time again between heavy rollers in the rolling mill. The mill consists really of a number of powerful mangles, which squeeze the metal flatter and flatter. Rolling can not only produce slabs and sheets of metals, but also shaped girders. Modern rolling mills work automatically under the control of a computer.

In forging, the red-hot metal is shaped by blows from a hammer. The blacksmith forges metal by hammering it by hand. In industry the metal is pounded by machinery. In the drop forge, for example, a heavy ram drops or is forced down on to the metal. It forces the metal into a cavity, or die, of the desired shape.

In a similar kind of process known as pressing, the metal is squeezed into shape gradually rather than suddenly. The presses which do this are massive machines which work by hydraulic (liquid) pressure. Some can press down with a force of tens of thousands of tons. They are used to squeeze red-hot ingots into such things as turbine shafts. Other hydraulic presses are used in the car industry, for example, to press cold sheet steel into body parts.

Other important metal-shaping processes include extrusion and drawing. In extrusion the metal is forced through the shaped holes of a die, and emerges as a shaped rod or tube. Toothpaste tubes, for example, are made by what is called impact extrusion. A soft metal alloy is hit so hard that it becomes plastic and flows through a die to form a tube. Wire is made by drawing (pulling) thin rods through smaller and smaller holes in a die.

Among more modern methods of shaping metal are power metallurgy and explosive forming. In powder metallurgy metal powders are pressed into molds and then heated fiercely. In explosive forming, the shock wave from an explosion is used to force metal into a mold.

Closed-die forging

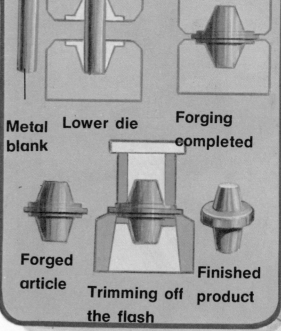

Upper die

Metal blank

Lower die

Forging completed

Forged article

Trimming off the flash

Finished product

Forging rolls

Tongs

Workpiece

Workpiece

Stop

Rolls have grooves which shape the component being forged. Each roll may carry a number of grooves, depending on what is to be produced.

Drop forge

Die

Control

Finished products

Machining

When a carpenter shapes a piece of wood, he uses carpentry tools like a drill, saw and plane. Similar kinds of tools are also used in industry to shape metal, but, because metal is so very much harder and tougher than wood, the tools must be driven by powerful machinery and be made of hard steel so that they cut well. These power-driven tools for metalworking are called machine tools.

One of the most common kinds of machine tool used in industry is the lathe. It is used for a cutting operation called turning. The workpiece – the piece of metal to be shaped – is placed in a clamp and rotated. Cutting tools are then moved in and remove metal from it. If the workpiece is long, the end is supported by the tailstock. A powerful electric motor in the headstock drives the lathe through a gearbox, which allows different speeds of rotation for different cutting operations.

The cutting tools are clamped in a tool post. This can be moved in several directions by means of a system of slides on the carriage or saddle. The position of the slides is adjusted by turning small handwheels. The saddle is generally moved by the feed shaft. A worm gear rotating with the feed shaft drives the saddle through a series of gearwheels. The gearwheels engage with a rack on the lathe bed and travel along it. The same worm gear also drives the cross slide.

The saddle can also be driven by the lead screw. It is clamped on to the lead screw by means of two half nuts, opened and closed by a control lever. When the nuts are closed, the rotating lead screw drives them and the saddle along.

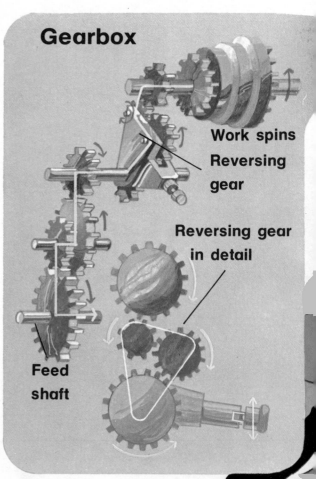

Gearbox

Work spins
Reversing gear

Reversing gear
in detail

Feed shaft

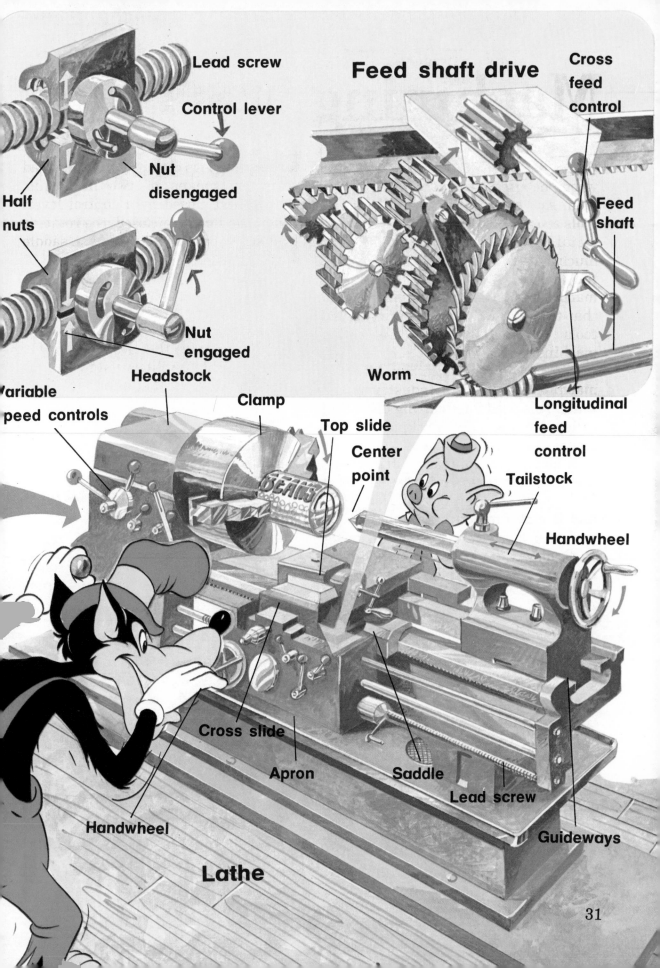

Lead screw

Control lever

Nut disengaged

Half nuts

Nut engaged

Variable speed controls

Headstock

Feed shaft drive

Cross feed control

Feed shaft

Worm

Longitudinal feed control

Clamp

Top slide

Center point

Tailstock

Handwheel

Cross slide

Apron

Saddle

Lead screw

Handwheel

Guideways

Lathe

Uneven wavemaking produces . . .

waves like ordinary light

Rhythmic wave making . . .

produces waves similar to laser light

Laser Cutting

One of the newest ways of shaping and cutting metals is by means of lasers. A laser is a machine that produces a narrow beam of pure light, which is so powerful that it can slice through metal or bore through diamonds as easy as winking. The word "laser" is short for a phrase that describes how it works – Light Amplification by Stimulated Emission of Radiation.

Flash lamp

Mirror

Ruby rod

Laser light

Drilling metal blocks

One kind of laser is the ruby laser. This is a ruby rod which has its ends silvered to act like mirrors. One of them is only half-silvered so that laser light can pass through. To start the laser, light from a powerful lamp is flashed on. Tiny atoms in the rod become excited and give off waves of pure red light. The waves strike other atoms and make, or stimulate, them into giving off more light of the same kind. Light traveling along the rod is reflected at the silvered ends and comes back to stimulate more and more atoms to give off the same pure light. The light rapidly gets stronger and stronger and then comes from the half-silvered end as a very powerful narrow beam, which can be focused for drilling and cutting.

The pictures on the left give an idea of the laser principle. In (1) the waves are being produced haphazardly. They are of all sizes and going in all directions. They are rather like the light waves coming from an ordinary light bulb. These are of different "sizes" (wavelengths, or colors) and going in all directions.

In (2) the waves are being made rhythmically. They have the same wavelength and travel in the same direction. Because of this, they become stronger and stronger.

The ruby laser only works in pulses. Other lasers work continuously, though they are not as powerful as the ruby laser. One of the most successful is the gas laser, which uses carbon dioxide gas. (This is the gas that forms the bubbles in fizzy drinks.) Another kind of laser uses materials similar to those used in transistors. They are called semiconductor lasers, but are not very powerful.

Gas laser

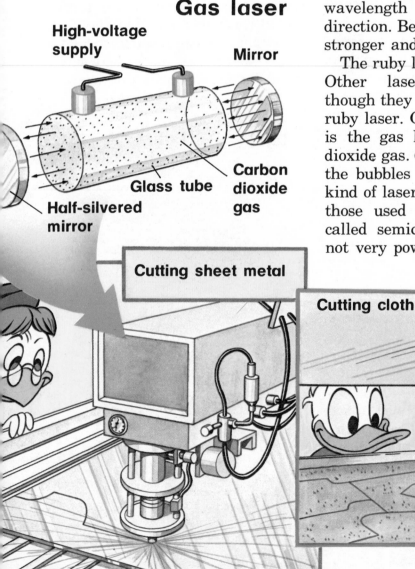

High-voltage supply

Mirror

Carbon dioxide gas

Glass tube

Half-silvered mirror

Cutting sheet metal

Cutting cloth

Metals Galore

Over 90 different chemical elements are found in nature. They are the "building blocks," which combine together in different ways to make the millions of different substances that exist on the earth, and some 70 of these chemical elements are metals. These are not often found as metals in the ground, but generally occur in minerals. To get metal, the minerals usually have to be smelted in furnaces.

A few metals can, however, be found in the form of a metal. They include gold and silver.

Copper can also sometimes be found as a metal in the ground, but most of our copper comes from minerals. Copper is one of the oldest metals known to man, and has been used since the beginning of civilization. Most copper today is used in electrical equipment because copper conducts (passes) electricity well.

Early man also used bronze. Bronze is a mixture of copper and another metal, tin. We call it an alloy of copper. Most metals are now used in the form of alloys.

Other copper alloys are brass and cupronickel. Brass is a mixture of copper and zinc. It has very many uses, from ornaments to shell cases. Cupronickel, a mixture of copper and nickel, is widely used for making coins.

The other metals mentioned above, tin and zinc, have other uses. They have one thing in common – they do not corrode, or rust easily. For this reason they are widely used as coatings on metals that do rust, such as iron and

steel. The "tin" cans used to store all manner of things are not actually made of all tin, but of steel plate coated with a thin layer of tin. When iron and steel are coated with zinc, the process is called galvanizing.

A form of rustproof steel can, however, be made by adding the metals chromium and nickel to iron. Most cutlery is made of stainless steel.

The other metal used very widely these days is aluminum. Its great advantage is that it is very light, and when it is made into an alloy, it can be as strong as steel. It conducts heat well, too, and that is one reason why it is used for making pots and pans.

At the Factory

A factory is a place where people group together to manufacture certain products. "Manufacture" means make on a large scale. The products may be anything from watch springs and nuts and bolts, to jet engines and motorcars.

Before there were factories, workers used to make products by hand in their homes. Their output was very low. Today workers look after machines which make the products, and output is hundreds of times faster.

Most products are made up of several parts, which have to be put together, to form a finished product. The advantage of using machines to make the parts is that they can produce identical parts every time. This means that the various parts will always fit each other when they are being assembled. This is the principle behind what is called mass production.

In the case of a simple product, such as a lawn mower, for example, a single person may assemble it from a pile of parts. In the case of a product such as a car, which consists of thousands of parts, a different method must be chosen. A common one is the assembly line method. This is illustrated on the following pages.

36

Bodywork

In the early days of motoring, every car was built lovingly by hand, one at a time, by skilled craftsmen. This was an expensive operation and took a long time. Then in the early 1900s American manufacturers introduced first the assembly line and then the moving conveyor into car making. The era of mass production began. Cars became cheap, especially in the United States where Henry Ford built his famous Model T, or "Tin Lizzie."

In a modern car factory, workers

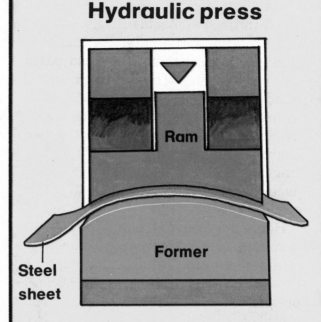

Hydraulic press

Ram

Former

Steel sheet

Pressing

Hydraulic press

Welding

Welding equipment

NUTS/BOLTS

stand in lines alongside a moving conveyor carrying the cars. As each car goes slowly past them, they add parts to it one at a time. The car may travel a hundred meters or more in this way before it is complete. The sequence in which assembly takes place varies slightly from factory to factory. The stages shown on this and the next pages will give you an idea of what goes on.

Here the body is being built and prepared. It is made from thin sheets of steel, which are pressed into shape by powerful hydraulic presses. These presses are so called because they use liquid (hydraulic) pressure to force down the ram on to the former.

After the sheets have been shaped, they are then joined together by welding. The welding torch heats up the metal parts to be joined, and molten metal may then be added. When the metal parts cool, they are strongly bonded together. Electric welding is generally done these days, and it may be carried out by robot welders.

The welded body is then dipped in a bath of rustproofing solution. This will help the body last longer. Afterward it is dipped in a primer, which is the first coat of paint. The car body then passes through a drying oven, after which it is sprayed with another coat of paint. It is again dried, and sprayed again. Several more coats of paint are applied in turn, finishing with the final glossy top coat.

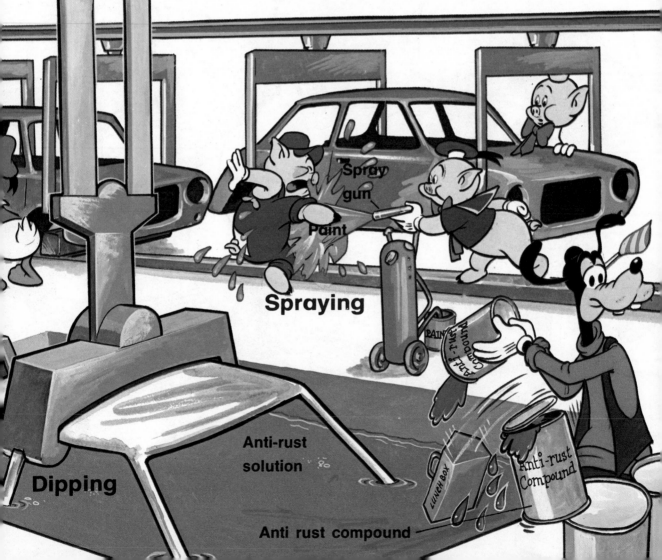

Taking Shape

While the car body is being built and painted in one section of the factory, the engine, transmission and other main parts of the car are being put together in another. A car factory is in fact a maze of assembly lines which build up individual parts into units, and then assemble these units into the finished vehicle. The lines are carefully controlled so that every part and every unit arrives at exactly the right place at exactly the right time. Computers are now used for this purpose.

The engine, for example, is built on a separate assembly line. The main engine block, which is usually made of cast iron, passes along a conveyor, and workers on either side add parts to it

Painted body shell

Wheel hub

Rear axle

one by one. Some of these parts are assembled on still other smaller assembly lines. The cylinder head, for example, is first fitted with valves, springs and rocker gear before it is bolted to the main engine block.

When the engine unit has been completed, it is carried by conveyor or traveling crane to the point on the main assembly line where it will be placed in position in the body. You can see an engine being fitted in this picture. The workers on the left are putting the finishing touches to the rear axle, to which the engine will soon be connected by the propeller shaft.

On some assembly lines the axles, wheels, suspension, steering and engine units are assembled on a chassis or frame, which is separate from the body. Most American cars, for example, have a separate chassis. When all these units have been assembled, the body shell, complete with windows and seats, is lowered on to the built-up chassis and secured.

Overhead conveyor

Traveling crane

Engine unit

Floor conveyor

The End of the Line

After the body, engine, transmission and wheels have been assembled together, the car looks almost ready, but there are still many things to be done. In particular the various parts of the electrical system must be installed and connected up. Often as much as 200 ft (60 meters) of electrical wiring are needed in a car.

Among the main electrical parts are the headlamps, sidelights, horn, generator, brake lights, starter motor, direction indicators, emergency flashers, battery, fusebox, rear lights, and instruments such as fuel gauge, oil-pressure gauge and ammeter. To make it easier to trace the different electrical circuits (paths), the connect-

Overhead conveyor

Faulty headlamp

Check list

Red paint

Floor conveyor

Inspector

ing wires are color-coded. This means that the plastic coatings over the wires are colored differently for different circuits.

Eventually, as it nears the end of the assembly line, the car is finished. Final adjustments are made to the steering system, tire pressures, and so on. The cooling system is filled with water, and oil is put into the engine. While these last minute operations are going on, inspectors check the overall appearance of the inside and outside of the car. If they find any faults, they bring in workers to correct them. If there are any blemishes on the paintwork, they bring in painters to touch them up. Fortunately, they do not often have the problem of painted cat paws!

At last the inspectors are satisfied, and another new car rolls off the assembly line. Mechanics then pour a few gallons of fuel into the car and start up the engine. They drive it on to a stationary test bed, and check that the engine and transmission — clutch, gearbox and final drive — work properly (see page 44).

New cars

Red paw prints

Testing, Testing

On the test bed the driving wheels of the new car rest on rollers. The car can then be "driven" without moving; the driving wheels simply turn the rollers. The wheel brakes and steering can also be tested on the rollers and adjusted if necessary.

Every so often one of the cars coming off the assembly line gets tested more thoroughly. For example, it may be placed in a shower room, which imitates heavy rainfall, to see if it leaks. It may be road tested on a test track to see if the brakes work properly in different conditions; if the suspension is soft enough; or if the steering is true. It may be taken on a skid pan, which is a slippery surface, to make

Test equipment

Electric motor

44 **Rotating rollers**

sure it handles well on wet and icy roads.

The testers may test some cars to destruction to see how well they will stand up to collisions. The inset picture below shows the result of one crash experiment. The testers paint reference lines on the side of the cars. By looking at these marks after the crash, they can see clearly how badly their cars have been damaged.

Car makers try to design their vehicles so that the front and rear ends collapse in a collision without affecting the "box" containing the driver and passengers. Car makers also crash cars containing dummies in place of real drivers. The dummies are wired with instruments so that the testers can calculate the forces involved in a crash. They also film the test crashes to see what happens to the dummies. The results from these experiments help car makers design safer cars.

Reference lines

Destructive testing

Brake testing

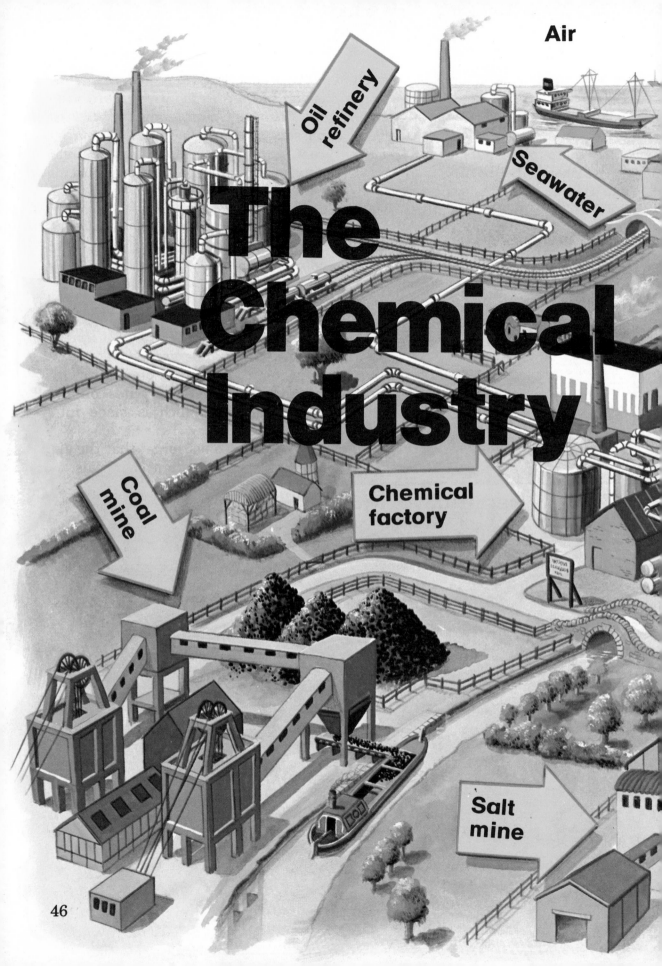

The Chemical Industry

Air

Oil refinery

Seawater

Coal mine

Chemical factory

Salt mine

46

Plastics, drugs, dyes, insecticides, aspirins, paint – these are just a few of the many different products made by the vast chemical industry.

To manufacture these chemicals requires many kinds of raw (basic) materials, lots of power, and all sorts of equipment, or "plant." The picture shows some of the typical raw materials needed by a chemical factory. The oil refinery supplies not only heating oil but also many basic chemicals. The coal mine also provides both fuel and raw materials.

A great many other raw materials are taken from the ground, like salt. Seawater contains not only salt, but other useful chemicals. Pyrites contain sulfur, most of which is made into sulfuric acid.

We must also not forget that the air contains very important chemicals.

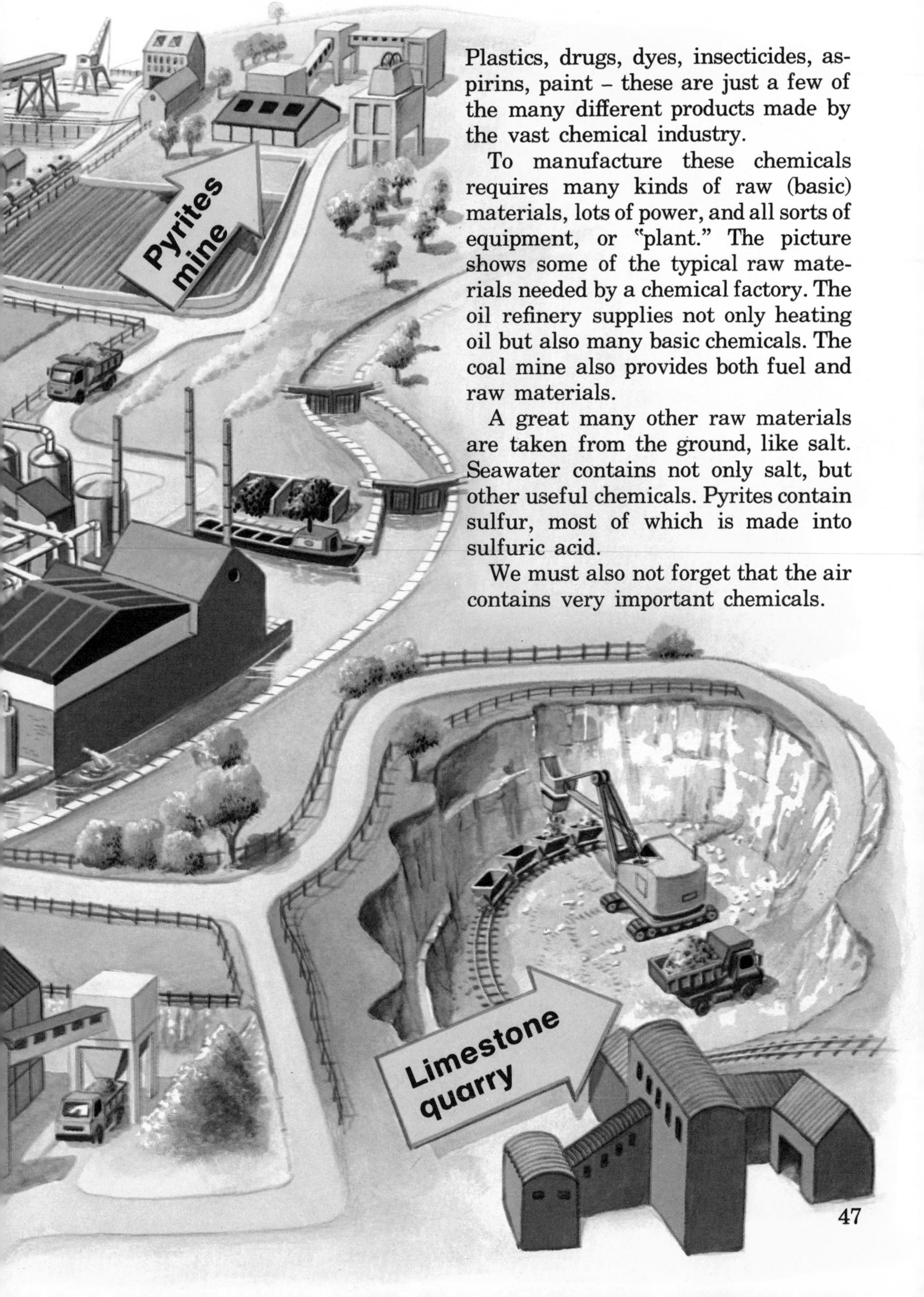

Pyrites mine

Limestone quarry

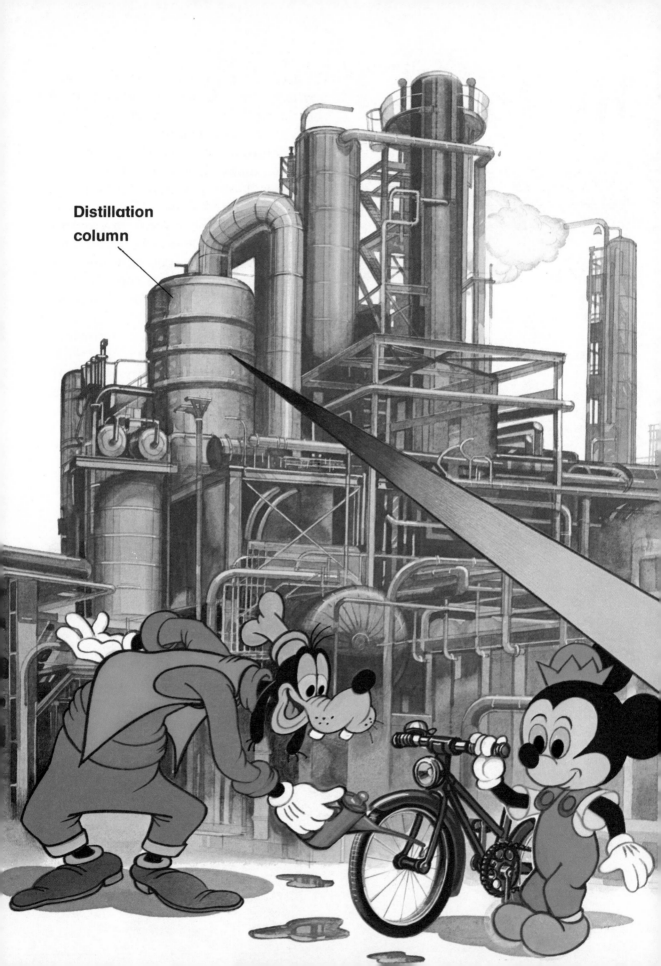

Distillation
column

Refining Crude Oil

Oil is one of the most precious raw (basic) materials in the world today. The trouble is that we are using so much oil that in the not too distant future supplies will run out. Oil as it comes from the ground is a thick greenish-black liquid. In this form it is called crude oil or petroleum. It is a mixture of hundreds of different chemicals containing the chemical elements hydrogen (H) and carbon (C). They are known as hydrocarbons.

By itself crude oil is of little use. It becomes valuable only when it is split up into its various chemicals. The separation process is known as refining and takes place in an oil refinery.

A modern oil refinery is made up of many tall steel towers and tanks connected by a maze of pipes. In the tall towers the main separation processes take place. They are the distillation towers. In these towers the crude oil is split into parts, or fractions, which each boil at a different temperature.

In distillation, crude oil is heated in a furnace until it turns into a vapor (gas). The vapor then goes to the distillation tower. In the tower there are trays of liquid oil fractions kept at different temperatures. As the vapor bubbles up through these trays the chemicals in the oil gradually separate out from it into the trays.

After passing through the distillation tower, the crude oil is separated into, for example, gasoline, kerosene, fuel oil and lubricating oil. Gasoline is taken off as vapor, which is later cooled to a liquid. The remainder are taken off as liquids from various levels of the tower.

Other processes take place in the oil refinery to make more of the oil into gasoline, because gasoline is the most valuable fraction. One process is called cracking. It is used to breakdown some of the heavier oils into lighter ones like gasoline. Another process does the reverse. It builds up light gases taken off from the top of the tower into more useful oils, including gasoline. Other processes at the refinery treat different petroleum fractions to produce chemicals with which to make plastics, detergents, dyes and many more such products.

Distillation

Vapor
Liquid
Gasoline vapors
Bubble cap
Kerosene
Distillation tower
Fuel oil
Furnace
Lubricating oil
Crude oil
High temperature
Residue

In the Chemical Laboratory

Complicated distillation apparatus

Apparatus stands

Microscope

Safety goggles

Test tube

Test tubes

Test tube stand

Tongs

Note pad

Laboratory assistant

Bunsen burner

Microscope slides

Most of the products of the chemical industry are made by bringing together different chemicals under certain conditions so that they react with one another. In a chemical reaction one chemical combines with another to form one or more other chemical products.

Glass tubing

Chief chemist

Bottles and jars of chemicals

Tap

Filter funnel

Filter paper

Flasks

Gas tap

Bench top

For example, soda (one chemical) undergoes a chemical reaction with hydrochloric acid (another chemical) to form salt (one chemical product) and the gas carbon dioxide (another chemical product).

At chemical factories engineers build equipment to carry out such chemical reactions on a large scale. First the reactions must be worked out in the laboratory by research chemists. Chemists carry out experiments to see how different chemicals react with one another. They are continually trying to find better chemical products – better plastics, dyes, insecticides, and so on – and better ways of making existing products.

The picture shows some of the basic equipment used in a chemical laboratory. Most of the equipment is made of heatproof glass. Glass is an excellent material for a laboratory because it is easy to shape into tubes, flasks, bulbs, bottles and so on. Also glass is a very inert material, which means that hardly any chemicals attack it, and, of course, glass is transparent, which makes it easy to see what is happening inside. Heatproof glass is needed because it is often necessary to heat substances so they react.

You can carry out simple experiments with materials in a test tube, either cold or hot. You heat it in the flame of a Bunsen burner. In a Bunsen burner, gas is mixed with more or less air before it is burned. This gives different heats. You alter the amount of air entering the burner by uncovering an air hole at the base. The burner is named after the famous chemist who invented it, Robert Bunsen.

The shelves of the laboratory are lined with jars containing all kinds of chemicals and bottles containing chemical solutions. Among the solutions are powerful acids such as hydrochloric, nitric and sulfuric acids. There are also powerful alkalis, such as ammonia and caustic soda. (Alkalis are the chemical opposites of acids.) There are also indicators such as litmus. Indicators are chemicals that become different colors in acid and in alkaline solutions.

It's a Plastic World

Among the most important products of the chemical industry are plastics. There are dozens of different plastics which we use in hundreds of different ways. The picture shows just a few of them. How many more things do you

Polythene film

Celluloid
ping-pong balls

PVC
tablecloth

Acetate bag

Acetate
scarf

Rayon shirt

Nylon
shirt

Synthetic
rubber soles

Heatproof Formica
surface

Polystyrene cups

Bakelite castors

know that are made of plastic?

Exactly what is a plastic? Broadly speaking, a plastic is something that is made up of chemicals with long molecules. It is also easy to shape. Many plastics are very waxy looking.

Polycarbonate bottles

Orlon hat

Polyester skirt

PVC shoes

This is not surprising because, like paraffin wax, many plastics come from petroleum (crude oil).

Because plastics have long molecules, they are usually quite flexible. Some are like rubber, which is a kind of natural plastic. One main group of plastics are known as thermoplastics. They are easily melted and shaped, and they can be remelted and reshaped time and time again. Our best-known plastics, nylon and polythene, are of this type.

Nylon has another useful property too. It can be drawn out into fine threads. We call it a synthetic fiber. We can make up nylon threads into cloth in the usual way (see pages 18/19). Polyester, orlon and acrilan are other common synthetic plastic fibers. Synthetic-fiber clothing is useful because it "drip-dries" very quickly. The plastic does not absorb water.

Another group of plastics are known as thermosetting plastics. They are shaped by heating, but in this case the heating sets them rigid and they cannot be remelted. They are heat-resistant. This makes them valuable for kitchen table tops, cups, plates, kettle handles, and so on. Bakelite, melamine and formica are among the best-known thermosetting plastics.

All of the plastics mentioned so far are made from petroleum chemicals, but plastic materials can also be made from natural sources – wood or cotton fibers. Wood and cotton contain cellulose, which has long molecules like the other plastics. By treating cellulose in different ways, plastics like celluloid, and man-made fibers like rayon and acetate can be produced.

53

Shaping Plastic

Plastics are substances that are easy to shape when they are hot, and there are many ways of shaping them. The most common are various methods of molding. Plastic bottles, toys such as dolls and other hollow articles are usually made by blow molding.

In blow molding, a tube of molten plastic is inserted into a mold of the required shape. Then a jet of air is blown into it. The air blows the plastic against the walls of the mold, which are water cooled. As the molten plastic touches the walls, it cools and freezes into shape. The mold then automatically splits open, and the molded object is removed.

Another common shaping process is injection molding. In this method hot plastic is forced into a shaped mold. The small diagram shows the kind of apparatus used. Plastic granules from a hopper are forced by a hydraulic ram

Blow molding

Plastic tube

Mold

along a cylinder. Heaters around the cylinder melt the plastic, which is then forced through a nozzle into a cooled mold. The plastic freezes into shape and is then removed.

Blow molding and injection molding are used for the thermoplastics, such as polythene and nylon, as is another process, called extrusion. In this process molten plastic is forced through a "die," or shaped hole. It is used to make plastic pipes and tubing, and also to make film. To make film, the die takes the form of a long narrow slot.

In an extrusion machine plastic granules are fed into a device similar to a kitchen mincer. They are heated so that they melt, and then the screw of the "mincer" moves the molten plastic forward and forces it through the die. The shaped plastic emerging from the die is then cooled by water.

Thermosetting plastics like bakelite and melamine cannot be shaped by the processes mentioned so far. This is because they set rigid when they are heated. These plastics must be heated and shaped in one operation. This is commonly done by compression molding. Plastic granules are placed in the lower half of a heated mold, and then the upper half of the mold is immediately forced down on top. The pressure makes the plastic flow, and the heat sets it.

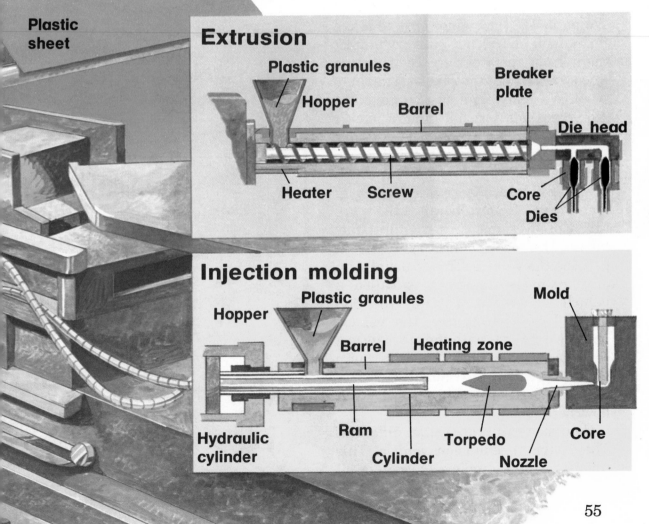

Plastic sheet

Extrusion

Plastic granules · Hopper · Barrel · Breaker plate · Die head · Heater · Screw · Core · Dies

Injection molding

Plastic granules · Hopper · Mold · Barrel · Heating zone · Hydraulic cylinder · Ram · Cylinder · Torpedo · Nozzle · Core

Mining the pigment

Making the vehicle

Paint chemist

Ball mill

Rotating cylinder

Rotating stone

Edge-runner mill

Paint Making

We paint our homes not only to make them look nicer, but also to protect them from the weather. By painting wood, we prevent the rain soaking in to rot it. We apply paint as a liquid, but it soon dries and forms a kind of plastic film.

Paint is made up of three main ingredients. One is the pigment, which gives the paint its color. Some pigments come from minerals; others are kinds of dyes made in chemical factories. The second main ingredient in paint is the vehicle. This is usually an oily, resinous liquid. It is called a vehicle because it "carries" the pigment. When paints dry, the vehicle usually combines with the air to form a solid protective film. The third main paint ingredient is thinner. This is a liquid added to the vehicle to make it flow better.

Emulsion paints are rather different. They have an emulsion vehicle. This consists of tiny droplets of resin or oil

56

in water. It is thinned simply with water. Emulsion paints are much easier to apply than oil paints, and afterwards your brushes can be cleaned simply in water.

To make paint, the pigment and vehicle are mixed together, and then the mixture is milled, or ground into a smooth paste. Milling takes place in ball mills and edge-runner mills. A ball mill is a huge rotating cylinder containing steel balls or pebbles. As the cylinder turns, the balls tumble over one another and grind the paint mixture between them. In the edge-runner mill the mixture is ground between a rotating grindstone and the bottom of the vessel.

When the pigment and vehicle are fully ground, they pass into a mixing tank. More vehicle is then added, together with the necessary thinners to bring the mixture to the right thickness. Additional pigments may also be added to make the paint exactly the right color.

Finally, the paint goes to an automatic filling machine, which pours a carefully measured amount into cans. The cans are then sealed with lids, labeled and packaged ready for distribution to stores.

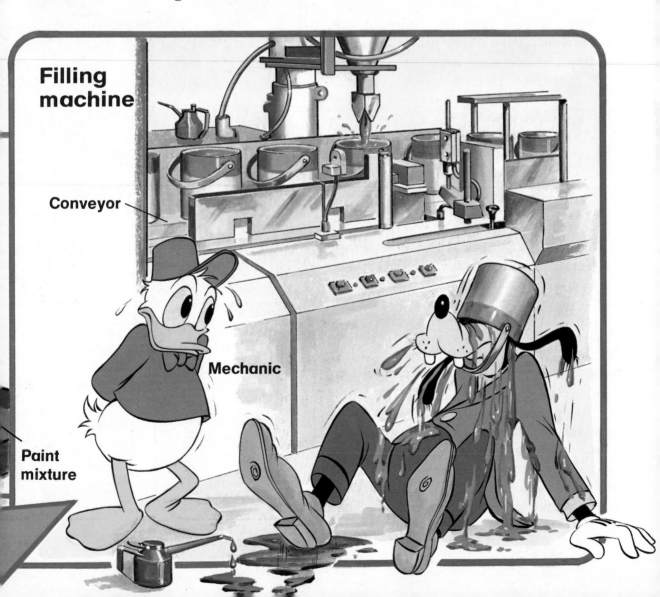

Filling machine

Conveyor

Mechanic

Paint mixture

Keeping Clean

To remain healthy we have to keep ourselves and our clothes as clean as possible. Germs breed where there is dirt. The oldest cleaning agent is soap which has been used for thousands of years. Soap is made by boiling up a mixture of oil or fat and caustic soda. Another useful substance, glycerine, is produced at the same time.

Soap is one kind of detergent, or cleansing agent. Many other kinds of detergents are now made from chemicals obtained from petroleum (crude oil). They are stronger in their action than ordinary soap.

All detergents work in a similar way. Their molecules have ends with different properties. One end is water-loving ("hydrophilic"); the other is water-hating ("hydrophobic"), or grease-loving (see picture 1).

When detergent is added to washing water, the water-hating "tails" of its molecules are attracted to any greasy dirt (2). Eventually the molecules completely surround the dirt so that only their water-loving ends are showing (3). This means that the dirt can now float away into the water (4), leaving the clothing fibers clean (5).

The water itself may affect the action of detergents, especially soap. This is illustrated in the main picture here. Sometimes the water contains minerals and is "hard." This means you cannot get a lather very easily. The

Hard water in

Water softener

Hard water – no lather

1 Water-loving part of molecule

Detergent action

Water-hating part of molecule

2 Detergent molecules attracted to dirt particle

Fiber

Grease

Soa

Sand

58

Drain

Automatic programmer

Inlet

Outlet

Ion-exchange resin

Filter

soap simply combines with the minerals to form a scum. However, the water can be treated, or softened, so that the offending minerals are removed.

In the usual kind of water softener the hard water is run through a bed of a special resin, called an oil-exchange resin. It is so called because it exchanges the mineral particles ("ions") that cause the hardness for other mineral particles that do not make water hard. From time to time the resin particles have to be treated so that they keep their softening action.

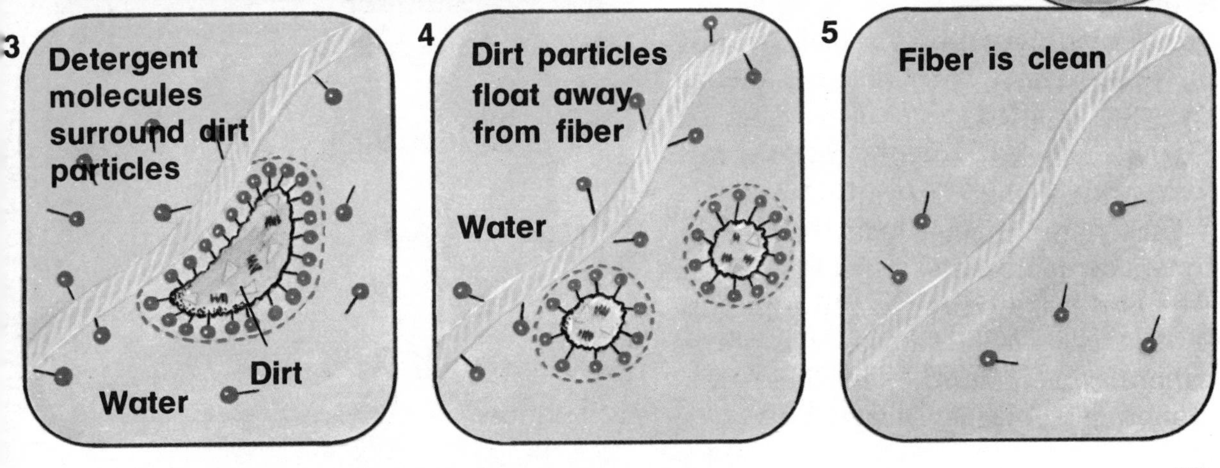

Soft water — good lather

3 Detergent molecules surround dirt particles

Water

Dirt

4 Dirt particles float away from fiber

Water

5 Fiber is clean

Danger: Blasting!

In many mining and construction operations large amounts of rocky material have to be broken up or removed. This is usually done by blasting with explosives. The first explosive used was gunpowder, a mixture of saltpeter, sulfur and charcoal. It was invented by the Chinese over 1,000 years ago and was the most powerful explosive known until dynamite came into use in the 1860s.

Dynamite is much more powerful than gunpowder, and is called a high explosive. It contains a substance called nitroglycerine, which by itself is extremely dangerous and explodes easily. In dynamite the nitroglycerine is absorbed in some material and becomes safer to handle. It then needs a small explosion to set it off. The device that provides this small explosion is called a detonator. There are several other high explosives, including TNT (trinitrotoluene). They all have to be detonated.

One kind of detonator used widely for blasting is shown here. It is also called a blasting cap. It is fired by electricity. Two electric wires lead to a thin "bridge wire" in the fusehead. When electricity is passed through it, the bridge wire heats up and ignites the materials around it. In turn this explodes small charges of explosive, which trigger off the high explosive.

The electric current needed to set off

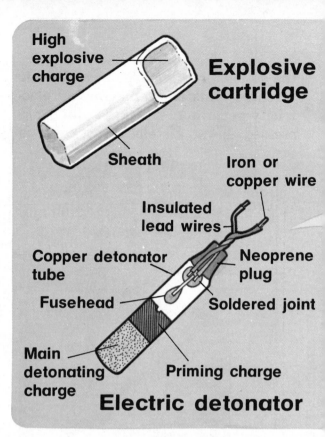

Explosive cartridge

High explosive charge

Sheath

Iron or copper wire

Insulated lead wires

Copper detonator tube

Fusehead

Neoprene plug

Soldered joint

Main detonating charge

Priming charge

Electric detonator

Plunger

Shotfirer

Blasting machine

the detonator is provided by a blasting machine. This is often a kind of electricity generator. When the plunger is pressed down, an electric current is produced, which fires the detonator.

Detonators can also be set off by a burning fuse. A fuse is a cord soaked in chemicals so that it burns at a steady rate. You light the end of a suitable length of fuse and head for cover. When the burning reaches the detonator, it and the charge explode.

In many blasting operations several sticks, or cartridges, of explosives are used and wired to the same blasting machine. To help the blasting action, the sticks are exploded at slightly different times, the middle one being exploded first. This is done by including special delay elements in the detonators, or by cutting fuses to different lengths.

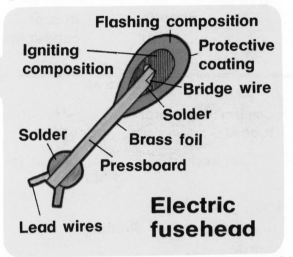

Flashing composition
Igniting composition
Protective coating
Bridge wire
Solder
Solder
Brass foil
Pressboard
Lead wires

Electric fusehead

Biplane

Landing gear
(Undercarriage)

F 6314

F 6314

Harrier
Jump Jet

Aircraft

The first airplane with an engine flew in 1903. It was made of wood, cloth and wire. It could reach a speed of only about 30 miles per hour (mph) and was able to stay in the air for only a few minutes at a time. Today sleek airplanes made of lightweight aluminum speed through the air at speeds of over 1,200 mph, and they can fly distances of 3,600 miles or more without stopping.

Airplanes are the commonest kind of aircraft – craft which fly through the air. Thousands of airplanes fly millions of miles every day, carrying passengers and cargo quickly and safely between airports in practically every country of the world.

Test pilot

Jet engine

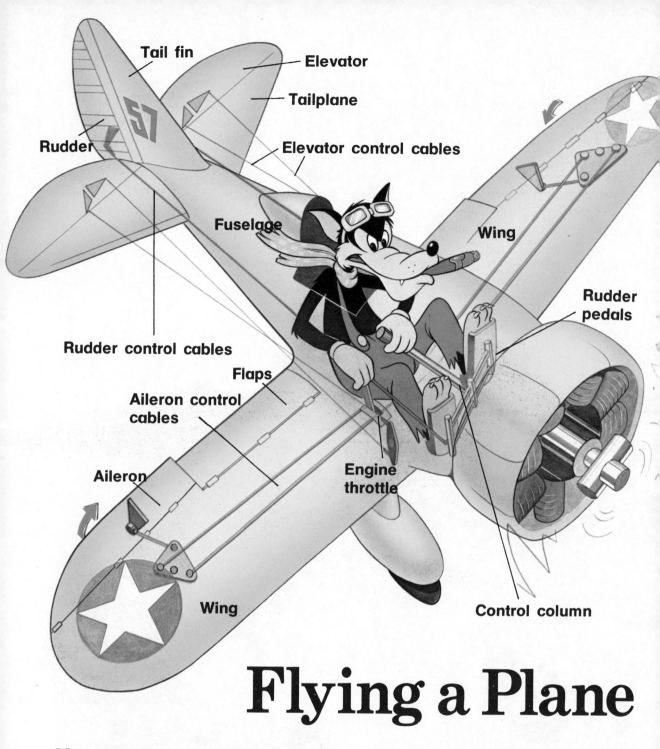

Tail fin

Elevator

Tailplane

Rudder

Elevator control cables

Fuselage

Wing

Rudder control cables

Rudder pedals

Flaps

Aileron control cables

Aileron

Engine throttle

Wing

Control column

Flying a Plane

Many people wonder how a plane, which is much heavier than air, can fly. The answer lies in its wings. The wings have a special shape. When they move through the air, they tend to lift.

It is the shape of the cross section of the wings which is important. The shape is called an airfoil. It is rounded in the front, curved at the top, but quite flat at the bottom. It tapers to a point at the rear. When an airfoil moves through the air, it experiences an upward force which we call lift. The faster the airfoil moves through the air, the greater is the lift. To take off, a plane travels faster and faster down the runway until the lift of its wings is greater than its own weight. Then it rises into the air.

As well as having wings, a plane must have a tail. The tail helps keep it flying steadily through the air in much the same way that the flight feathers of an arrow make it travel straight. The vertical (upright) part of the tail is called the tail fin. The horizontal (level) part of the tail is called the tailplane.

When a plane is airborne, the pilot controls it by means of a control column and foot pedals. These controls move panels ("control surfaces") on the tail and on the wings which deflect the air in different directions.

The control surfaces and controls of a simple plane are shown in the large picture. In this plane the surfaces are moved by cables. In most planes these days the surfaces are moved by hydraulic (liquid) pressure, just like the brakes of a car.

By moving the control column to the left, or right, the pilot operates the ailerons on the rear, outer edge of the wings. As one aileron goes up, the other goes down. This makes the wings of the plane dip up and down.

By moving the control column backward or forward, the pilot moves the elevators on the tailplane up or down. By pressing on the foot pedals, left or right, the pilot moves the rudder on the tail fin left or right. To make a controlled turn, or climb, or descend, the pilot generally uses the engine throttle as well, to speed up or slow down the plane.

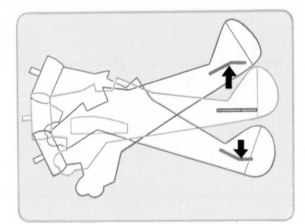

Elevator down pushes tail up
Elevator up pushes tail down

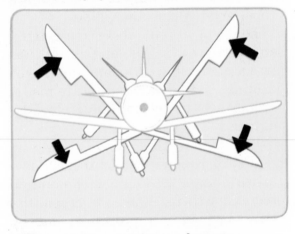

Aileron down pushes wing up
Aileron up pushes wing down

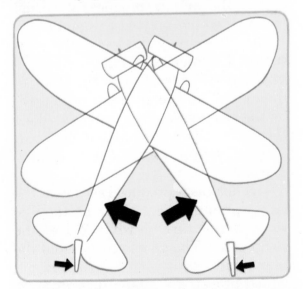

Moving rudder right swings plane right
Moving rudder left swings plane left

Flying Power

To get enough speed to fly, planes must have powerful engines. In the early days of flying, all planes had piston engines. Today only a few light planes have this kind of engine, which spins a propeller to propel the plane.

The piston engine works in much the same way as a car engine. It has pistons moving in cylinders, and burns gasoline as fuel. Most aircraft piston engines are air-cooled, like motorbike engines.

Most planes these days, however, have a different kind of engine, called a gas-turbine, or jet engine. The engine produces a thrust (force) to propel the plane, not with a propeller, but by means of a jet, or stream of gases. The force of the gases shooting backward out of the engine produces a thrust forward, which propels the plane.

The diagram at the top of the page shows a simple jet engine, called a turbojet. Air is sucked in the front of the engine and compressed (squeezed) by the compressor. The compressed air then goes into a combustion chamber. Fuel is sprayed into it and is ignited (burned).

The hot gases produced escape at the rear, spinning the turbine as they do so. It is this turbine which drives the compressor. The gases escape from the rear nozzle as a very high speed jet, which propels the plane forward.

In practice the compressor and tur-

Compress[or]

Air intake

Fixed blades

Movi[ng] blade[s]

Connecting rods

Propeller shaft

Piston

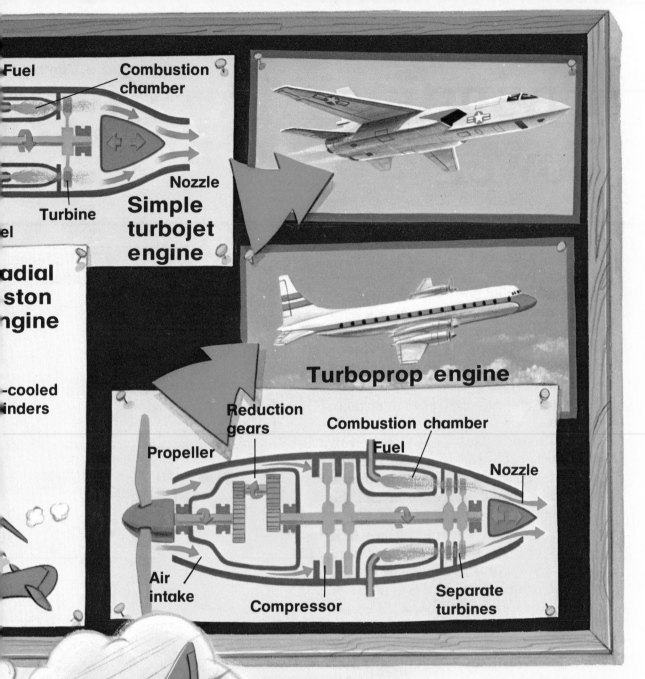

Fuel

Combustion chamber

Nozzle

Turbine

Simple turbojet engine

adial
ston
ngine

-cooled
inders

Turboprop engine

Reduction gears

Propeller

Combustion chamber

Fuel

Nozzle

Air intake

Compressor

Separate turbines

bines are divided up into several sections, or stages, which makes them more efficient. One, called a turbofan, has a huge fan at the front which adds a stream of cold air to the jet.

The type of jet engine known as a turboprop, also uses a propeller for propulsion. It is shown in the diagram above. It has two separate turbines. One drives the compressor, and the other drives the propeller.

67

Designing Aircraft

Aircraft of many shapes and sizes fly through the skies. The shape they have did not come about by accident but is the result of careful design and experiment. The shape chosen for a plane depends a great deal on the speed at which it will fly.

The shape is important because of air resistance, or drag. Any object traveling through the air experiences drag, and the faster it travels, the more drag there is. A plane must be shaped so as to have as little drag as possible. Then its engines can propel it more efficiently. The diagrams on sheet 7 on the bulletin board here show this vividly.

A circular plate placed in a high-speed air stream may have a drag equivalent to the pull of 20 men (A). A ball of the same diameter has only half the drag (B). The specially shaped body in (C) has only one-twentieth of the origianl drag. This body has what is called a streamlined shape. Streamlining is very important in aircraft design.

The ideal streamlined shape depends on the air speed. For low speeds the shape is like a fish's body. For high speeds it is much narrower and more pointed. That is why low-speed planes can have bulbous bodies, but very high-speed planes must have slender bodies and a pointed nose.

The shape of the wing also needs to be altered as the design speed increases. Low-speed transport planes (2) can have wings that stick out at

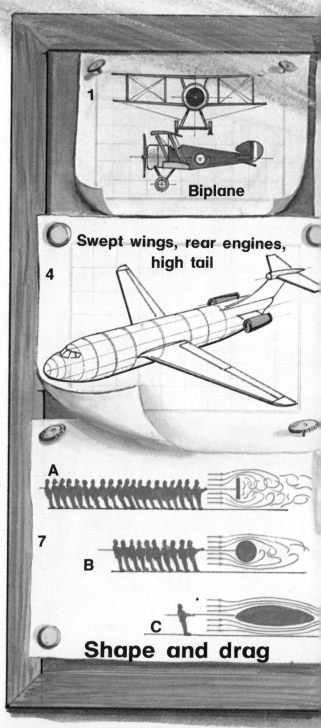

1 Biplane

4 Swept wings, rear engines, high tail

A

7

B

C

Shape and drag

right angles, but higher speed jet airliners (3 and 4) must have their wings swept back at an angle. Then they can travel at speeds up to about 600 mph (960 km/h) without difficulty.

If a plane travels much faster than this, it approaches the speed of sound, and then strange things start to happen. The airflow over its body begins to break down, and shock waves form. This causes the plane to vibrate and be buffetted about. This effect can be reduced by designing the plane with a triangular, or delta wing (5). The supersonic airliner Concorde has a delta wing. "Supersonic" means that it can travel faster than the speed of sound.

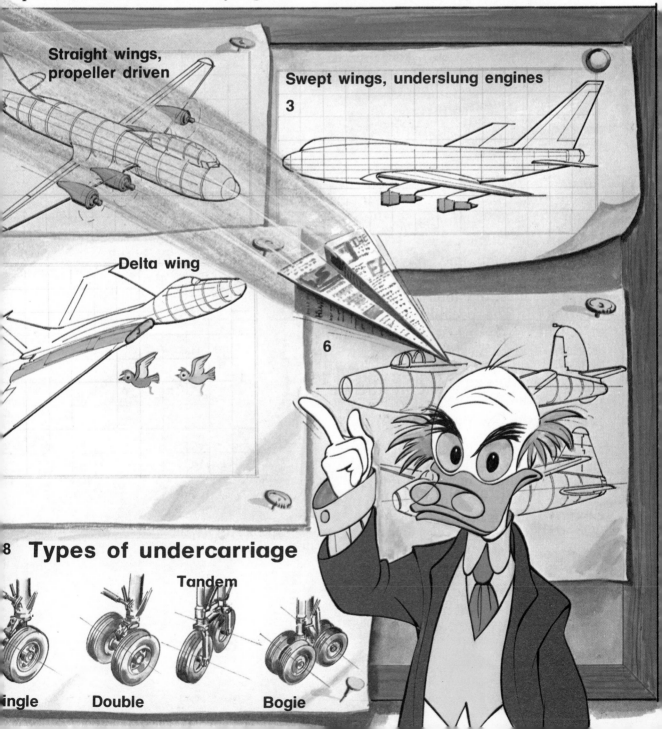

Straight wings, propeller driven

Swept wings, underslung engines

3

Delta wing

6

8 **Types of undercarriage**

Tandem

ingle **Double** **Bogie**

Wind Tunnels

Designing and building a plane takes a long time and is very expensive. A designer cannot just build one and then see how well it flies. He must know beforehand how well his plane will behave. He finds this out by experimenting with scale models of his design in a wind tunnel.

The aircraft designer suspends the model from balances, which are sensitive weighing scales. The balances measure the forces acting upon the model when it is "flying." He may introduce streams of smoke into the tunnel to see how the air flows past the model. Or he can see how the air flows by means of special photography.

From all his measurements and photographs for different air speeds past the model, the aircraft designer gets a good idea of how a full-size plane will behave in real flight. He keeps changing his design until he is satisfied that it is the best one for the purpose. Then he can go ahead and draw up detailed plans, from which the full-size plane will be built.

There are a number of different kinds of wind tunnels, each designed for different speeds of air flow. The ones designed for air speed below the speed of sound are called subsonic tunnels. Those designed for speeds greater than the speed of sound are called supersonic tunnels. Those designed for speeds in between are called transonic tunnels.

Engine exhaust silencer

Air intake

Suspension wires

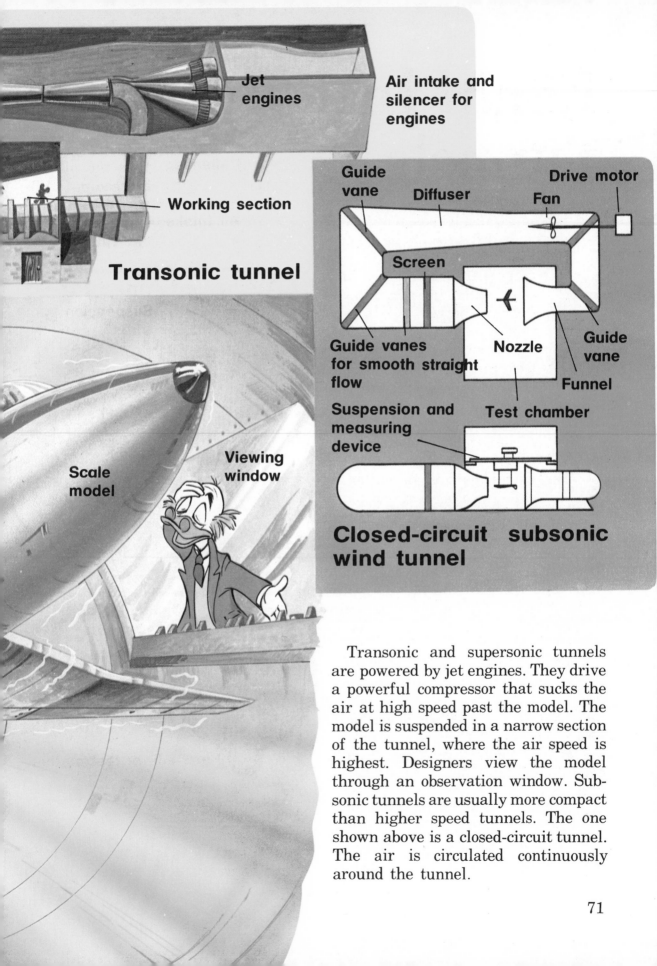

Jet engines

Air intake and silencer for engines

Working section

Transonic tunnel

Guide vane

Diffuser

Drive motor

Fan

Screen

Guide vanes for smooth straight flow

Nozzle

Guide vane

Funnel

Suspension and measuring device

Test chamber

Closed-circuit subsonic wind tunnel

Scale model

Viewing window

Transonic and supersonic tunnels are powered by jet engines. They drive a powerful compressor that sucks the air at high speed past the model. The model is suspended in a narrow section of the tunnel, where the air speed is highest. Designers view the model through an observation window. Subsonic tunnels are usually more compact than higher speed tunnels. The one shown above is a closed-circuit tunnel. The air is circulated continuously around the tunnel.

Flight Instruments

In the cockpit of an aircraft there are all manner of dials and instruments which help the pilot to fly. Some tell him how the plane's engines are working, how much fuel he has, how fast he is flying, in which direction he is heading, and so on. Four of the most important instruments are the air speed indicator, the altimeter, the gyrocompass and the artificial horizon.

The air speed indicator is the plane's speedometer. It measures how fast the plane is traveling through the air. To find how fast it is traveling over the ground beneath, the pilot has to add or subtract the speed of the wind.

The indicator takes the form of a pair of concentric tubes (one inside the other). The middle tube faces the air stream, while the other is connected to holes facing sideways ("static" holes). When the indicator moves through the air, there is a difference in pressure between the air forced into the middle tube and the air entering the static holes. This difference in pressure causes the hollow diaphragm to change size. These changes are made to move the pointers over a speed scale.

The plane's altimeter measures how high it is. The simplest one works by means of air pressure, which gradually drops as you go higher, so this altimeter is a kind of barometer. It has a container from which most of the air has been removed. The container expands as the air pressure drops. This movement moves the pointer of the altimeter. Most planes now, however, have radio altimeters, which work by

bouncing radio waves off the ground.

The gyrocompass tells the pilot in what direction he is heading. It is better than a magnetic compass because it is not affected by magnetic disturbances. The card carrying the

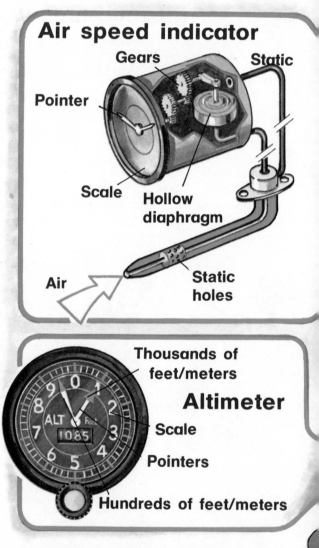

Air speed indicator

Gears — Static — Pointer — Scale — Hollow diaphragm — Static holes — Air

Altimeter

Thousands of feet/meters — Scale — Pointers — Hundreds of feet/meters — ALT — 1085

compass headings is connected to a gyroscope, which always points in the same direction, no matter how the plane twists and turns.

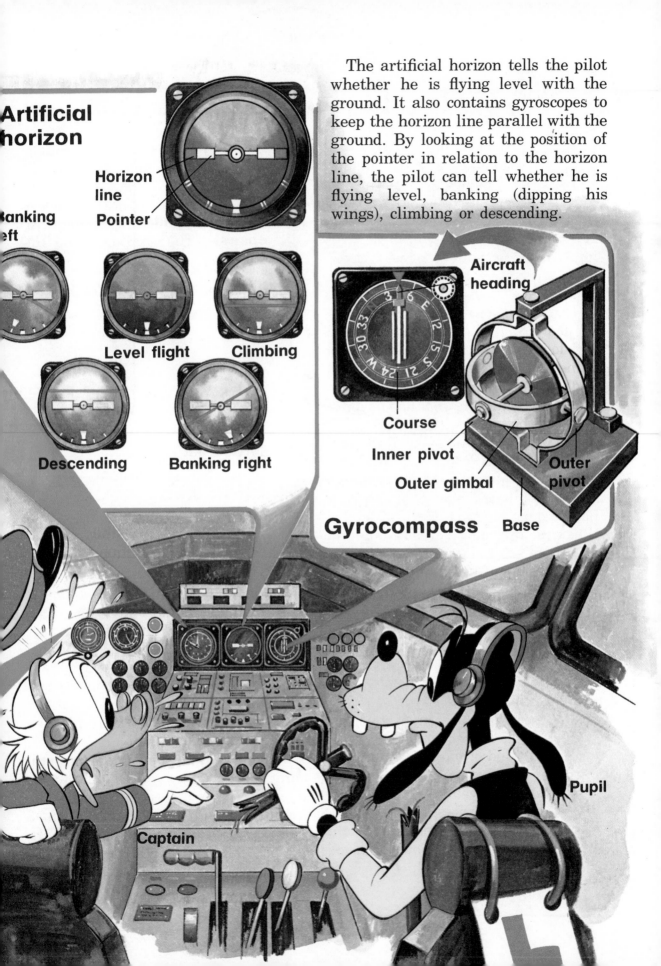

Artificial horizon

Horizon line

Pointer

Banking left

Level flight

Climbing

Descending

Banking right

The artificial horizon tells the pilot whether he is flying level with the ground. It also contains gyroscopes to keep the horizon line parallel with the ground. By looking at the position of the pointer in relation to the horizon line, the pilot can tell whether he is flying level, banking (dipping his wings), climbing or descending.

Aircraft heading

Course

Inner pivot

Outer gimbal

Outer pivot

Gyrocompass

Base

Captain

Pupil

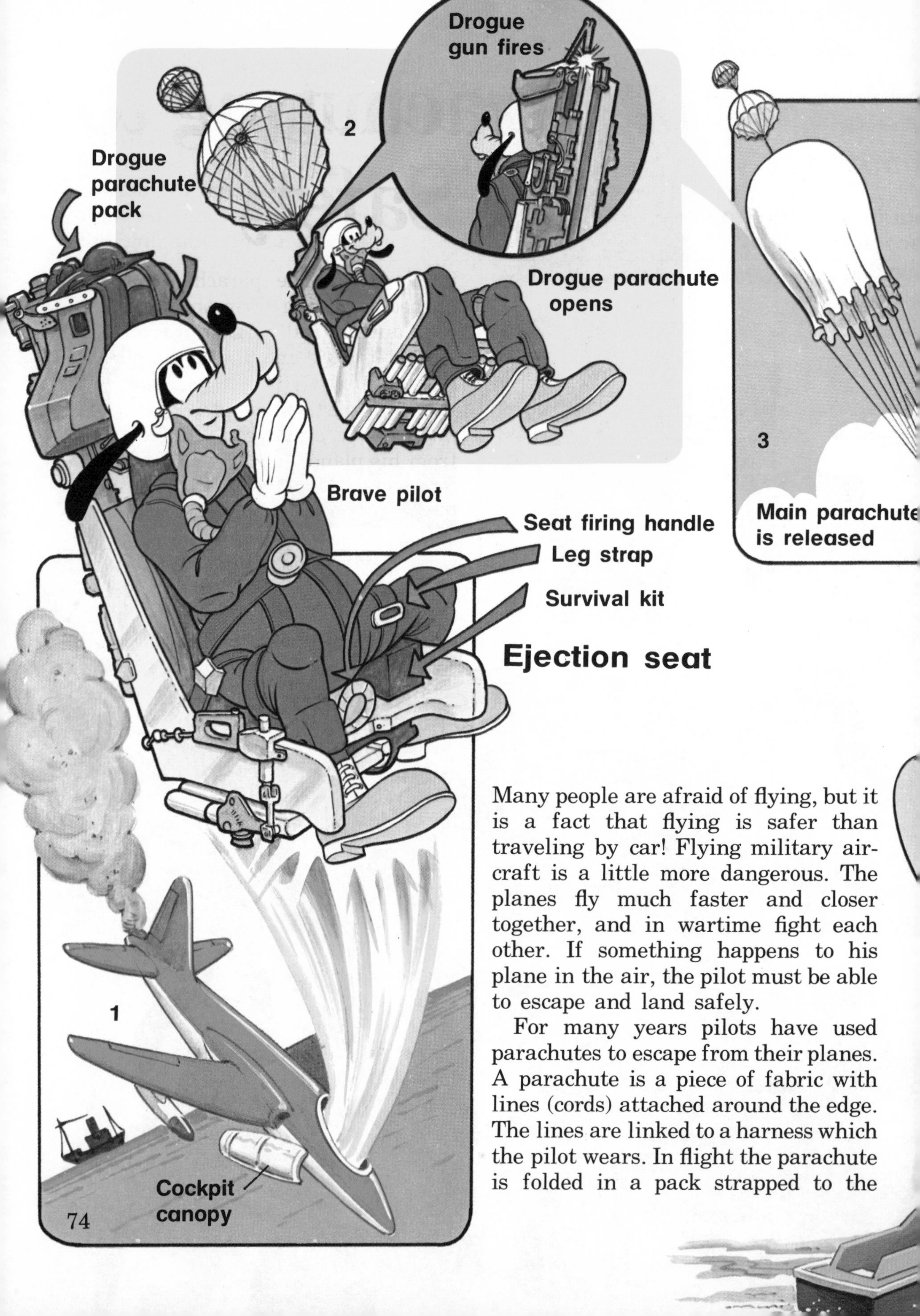

Drogue gun fires

2

Drogue parachute pack

Drogue parachute opens

Brave pilot

Seat firing handle

Leg strap

Survival kit

Ejection seat

3

Main parachute is released

1

Cockpit canopy

Many people are afraid of flying, but it is a fact that flying is safer than traveling by car! Flying military aircraft is a little more dangerous. The planes fly much faster and closer together, and in wartime fight each other. If something happens to his plane in the air, the pilot must be able to escape and land safely.

For many years pilots have used parachutes to escape from their planes. A parachute is a piece of fabric with lines (cords) attached around the edge. The lines are linked to a harness which the pilot wears. In flight the parachute is folded in a pack strapped to the

Nylon canopy

at is
scarded

Lines

Harness

4

**Rescue
launch**

Parachuting to Safety

pilot's body. The parachute can be opened by pulling a "ripcord," or it may open automatically. When it is open, it catches the air and allows the pilot to fall quite slowly.

In the past, when planes traveled more slowly, a pilot could simply jump from his plane, and then pull the ripcord when he was clear. Now, however, planes travel so fast that a pilot cannot get out so easily, so his plane is fitted with an ejection seat. This seat is ejected from the plane by a small rocket when the pilot pulls the firing handle.

The rocket will blast the seat clear, and then small "drogue" parachutes open as the pilot begins to descend. The seat is then discarded, and the main parachute opens and lets the pilot float gently back to earth. The parachute opens automatically.

Parachuting is not only done in emergencies. It has become quite a popular sport. The most exciting form of this sport is skydiving. Parachutists jump from a plane, but do not open their parachutes immediately. They drop through the air in what is called "free fall." They can perform spins and rolls and join up with other skydivers until they have to open their parachutes. Different types of parachutes are used in sport parachuting, enabling the jumpers to control their speed and direction.

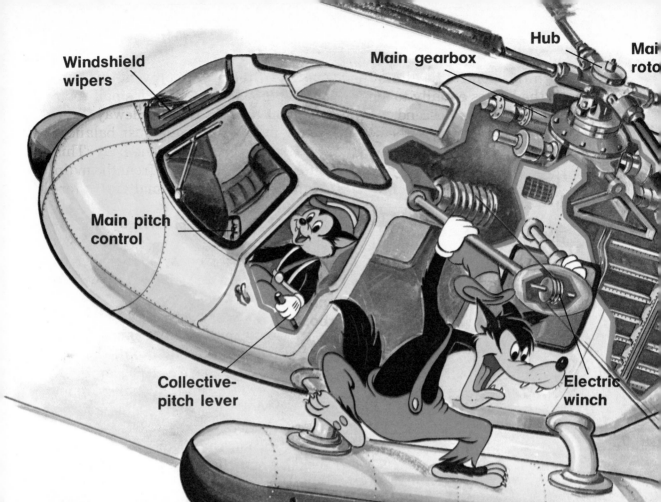

Windshield wipers

Main gearbox

Hub

Main rotor

Main pitch control

Collective-pitch lever

Electric winch

Float landing gear

Perfect Flight

Ordinary planes can travel very fast and carry many people, but they need a very long runway on which to take off and land, and they cannot maneuver very easily in the air. Another kind of aircraft can take off and land in very little space, and can twist and turn with ease. It can fly sideways and backward and even hover motionless in the air like a fly. This aircraft is the helicopter.

The helicopter does not have ordinary wings like a plane. It has a rotary wing, or rotor. The rotor is made up of several blades. When these blades

turn, they produce a lifting force which supports the helicopter's weight. This is similar to what a wing does when it travels through the air (page 64). In many helicopters today the rotor is driven by gas-turbine engines, through a gearbox.

The rotor blades not only lift the helicopter into the air. They also propel it. The pilot can make the helicopter fly in a particular direction by altering the angle, or pitch of each of the rotor blades. He does this by means of a pitch-control column. The other main control he has is the collective-pitch

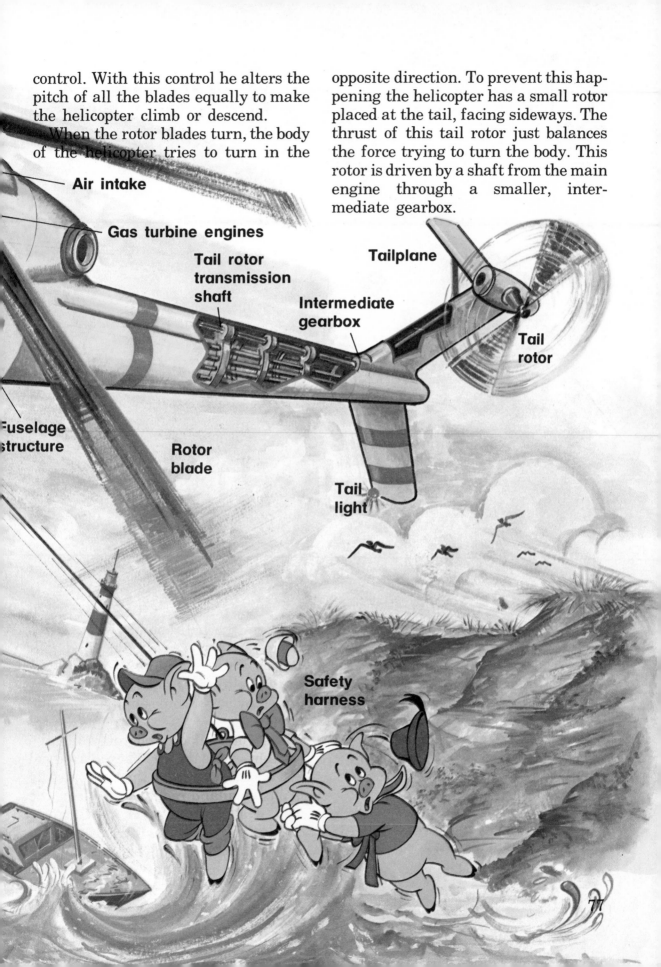

control. With this control he alters the pitch of all the blades equally to make the helicopter climb or descend.

When the rotor blades turn, the body of the helicopter tries to turn in the opposite direction. To prevent this happening the helicopter has a small rotor placed at the tail, facing sideways. The thrust of this tail rotor just balances the force trying to turn the body. This rotor is driven by a shaft from the main engine through a smaller, intermediate gearbox.

Air intake

Gas turbine engines

Tail rotor transmission shaft

Tailplane

Intermediate gearbox

Tail rotor

Fuselage structure

Rotor blade

Tail light

Safety harness

Paper

The Chinese first discovered how to make paper nearly 2,000 years ago. They were also, much later, the first people to print from movable type. Paper making and printing are two of the most important inventions man has made. They have enabled us to produce books and newspapers, for example, in great quantities. As a result everybody can be better educated. They can learn about past and present local and world news, and about any subject that interests them, from astronomy and baseball to yoga and zebras.

Printing and Packaging

Preparing the Pulp

Most paper starts its life in the forest. It is prepared from woodpulp obtained from felled trees. All kinds of trees are used, including firs, spruce, pine and poplar. After the trees have been felled, they are cut up into handy-sized logs, which then go to the pulp mill. At the mill the logs go first into a machine called a log debarker, which removes the bark from them. Then they are made into pulp in one of two ways.

In one method, they are ground up by a revolving grindstone, which is cooled by water to prevent overheating. The grindstone breaks up the wood into fine fibers that mix with the cooling water to form pulp, which looks rather like runny paste. A screen (sieve) removes coarse pieces and the hard knots.

In the other main method of preparing pulp, the logs are shredded into chips and "cooked" under pressure with chemicals in a huge tank called a digester. The pressure cooking process separates the wood fibers. After cooking, the liquid pulp mass is thoroughly washed, then bleached white, and washed again.

The pulp mills are usually located in the forest regions, whereas the paper mills may be hundreds of miles away, so the pulp is usually dried into sheets, which are transported to the paper mills.

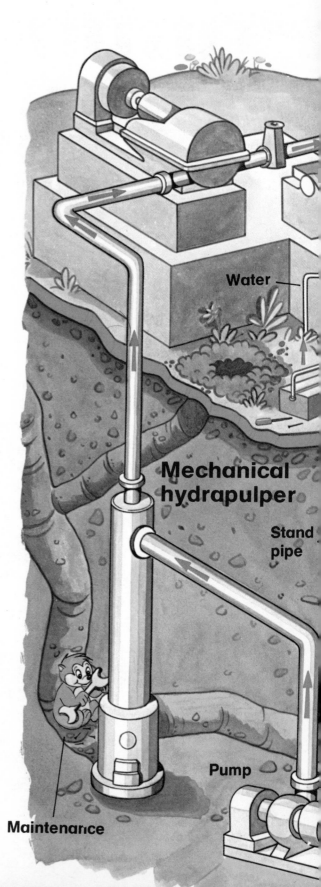

Water

Mechanical hydrapulper

Stand pipe

Pump

Maintenance

The first job to do at the paper mill is to convert the dry sheets of pulp back into liquid pulp. This is done in a machine called a hydrapulper. It is a large open tank in which the pulp sheets are mixed with water. An agitator stirs the mixture, helping to break down the sheets into separate fibers. The liquid pulp is circulated through screens to remove oversize lumps before being pumped for further processing.

Vibrating screen

Rejects

Junk remover

Ragger

Assistants

Pulp

To beating machine

Liquid pulp

Pump

81

From Pulp to Paper

Suction rollers

Couch rolls

Breast box   Liquid pulp

Wet pulp

Wire-mesh belt

Damp paper web

Wet end

The liquid pulp from the hydrapulper is not yet ready to be made into paper. First it goes into a beating machine in which beater bars pound it to refine and fray the wood fiber. From the beater the refined pulp goes into a mixing tank, where other materials are added to it. Such materials include clay and sizing (a kind of glue). They make the resulting paper smoother and

82

easier to write on. Colored dyes or pigments may also be added to color the paper.

After thorough mixing with the additional ingredients, the pulp is ready for the paper-making machine. This is a huge machine which may be up to 330 ft (100 meters) long. The liquid pulp first enters the breast box at the "wet end" of the machine. From there it flows on to a fast-moving belt made of fine wire mesh.

The water drains through the belt as the pulp moves along. Then suction boxes or rollers suck more water from the pulp layer until it becomes a damp paper "web." Several sets of rollers help squeeze more water from the web before it is fed around a series of drying cylinders, which are heated by steam.

The dry paper emerging from the cylinders is then passed through a series of heavy "calender" rollers. Calendering gives the paper a smooth, firm surface. Finally, the paper is wound onto a reel at a rate of nearly 25 mph (40 km/h).

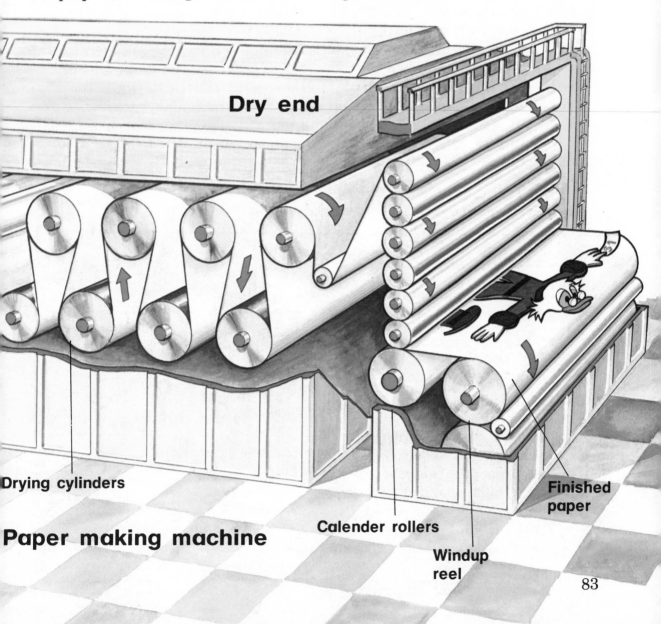

Dry end

Drying cylinders

Paper making machine

Calender rollers

Windup reel

Finished paper

Printing Processes

In the process of printing, an image is made on paper from an inked plate. There are three main methods of printing, each of which uses a different kind of printing plate.

The oldest method of printing uses a printing plate which has a raised printing surface. It is called letterpress (see diagram A). Diagrams B and C show the working principles of a flatbed cylinder printing press. The printing plate, or forme, is held in a flat "bed." The bed moves back and forth. As it moves one way, the printing plate is inked. As it moves the other way, it passes beneath the impression cylinder which presses the paper against the inked plate.

Faster printing can be done on a rotary press, which prints from curved printing plates (D).

The second main printing method used today is offset litho. "Litho" is short for lithography, a method of printing from a flat surface (E). It works on the principle that grease and water do not mix. The printing plate is prepared and treated photographically so that the printing areas repel water but attract the greasy printing ink.

The basic processes in litho printing are shown in diagram F. The printing plate is dampened, wetting all the surface except the type image (2). When the plate is inked, the ink stays only on the type image (3), being repelled by the rest of the wet surface. The plate will thus print only from the type area (4-6). A litho press (G) has a plate cylinder which carries an inked image first on to a blanket cylinder. The

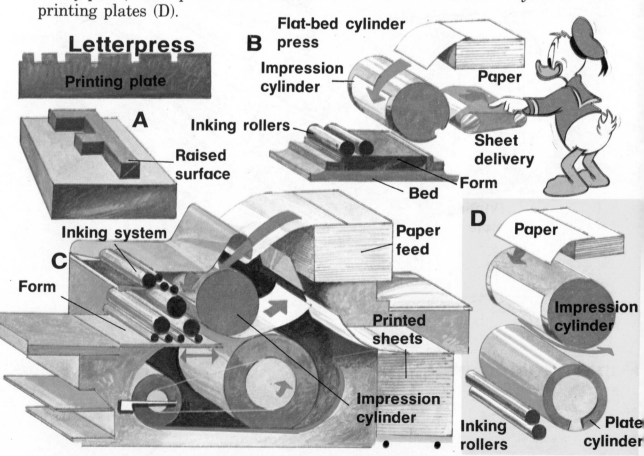

Letterpress

Printing plate

A

Raised surface

Inking system

C

Form

B **Flat-bed cylinder press**

Impression cylinder

Inking rollers

Bed

Form

Paper

Sheet delivery

Paper feed

Printed sheets

Impression cylinder

D

Paper

Impression cylinder

Inking rollers

Plate cylinder

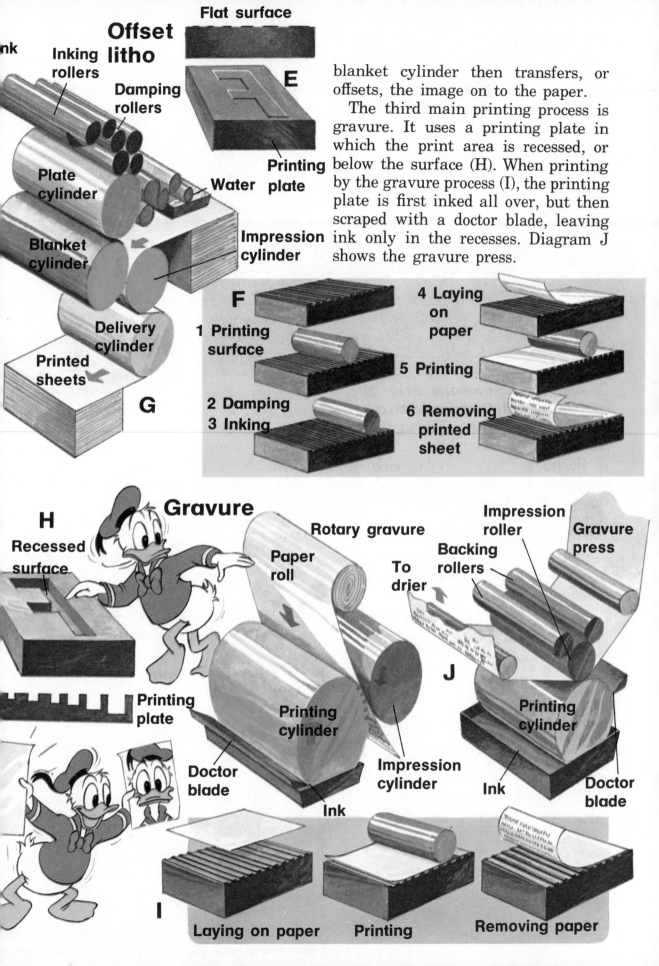

Offset litho

Flat surface

nk

Inking rollers

Damping rollers

E

Printing plate

Water

Plate cylinder

Blanket cylinder

Impression cylinder

Delivery cylinder

Printed sheets

G

blanket cylinder then transfers, or offsets, the image on to the paper.

The third main printing process is gravure. It uses a printing plate in which the print area is recessed, or below the surface (H). When printing by the gravure process (I), the printing plate is first inked all over, but then scraped with a doctor blade, leaving ink only in the recesses. Diagram J shows the gravure press.

F

1 Printing surface

2 Damping
3 Inking

4 Laying on paper

5 Printing

6 Removing printed sheet

Gravure

H

Recessed surface

Printing plate

Doctor blade

Rotary gravure

Paper roll

To drier

Printing cylinder

Ink

Impression cylinder

Impression roller

Gravure press

Backing rollers

J

Printing cylinder

Ink

Doctor blade

I

Laying on paper

Printing

Removing paper

Writing and editing

Editor
Copy
Reporter

Typesetti

Keyboard
operator

Producing a daily newspaper is a hectic business. Work of some kind or another goes on 24 hours a day. Reporters chase here, there and everywhere reporting local and international news and searching for other interesting "feature" stories. They write up their news items or stories back in the newspaper office, or they phone in their articles to the office if they are far away.

At the office the articles are edited by "subs" (sub-editors) into their final form. This final "copy" is then sent for typesetting. This is usually done on a Linotype machine, which sets the copy line by line. The operator taps out the copy on a keyboard. For each letter he taps, a tiny type mold, or matrix, drops into line. When a line of matrixes is complete, hot metal is poured into them. This cools and sets hard as a complete line, or slug, of type.

The lines drop into place in a holder, often called a galley. An inked impression, or galley proof, is then taken of them.

The different batches of type are

then made up into page units, and printing plates are made from them. The plates are then fitted to the printing cylinders on the high-speed rotary presses.

Producing Newspapers

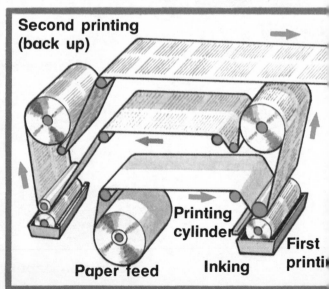

Second printing (back up)

Printing cylinder

Paper feed

Inking

First printi

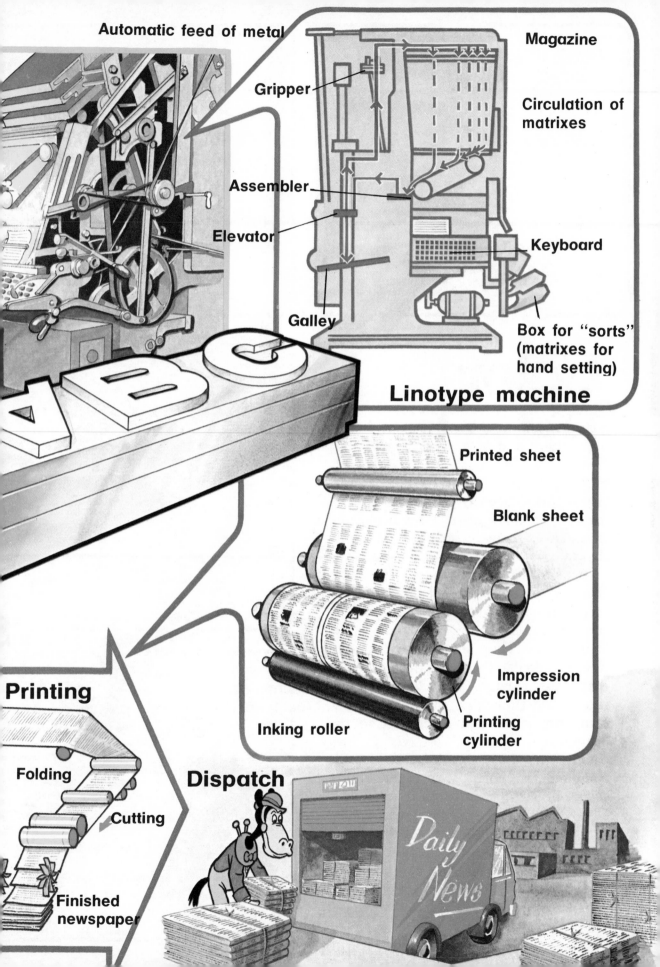

Automatic feed of metal

Magazine

Gripper

Circulation of matrixes

Assembler

Elevator

Keyboard

Galley

Box for "sorts" (matrixes for hand setting)

Linotype machine

Printed sheet

Blank sheet

Impression cylinder

Printing cylinder

Inking roller

Printing

Folding

Cutting

Finished newspaper

Dispatch

Daily News

Yellow

Magenta

Yellow and magenta

Yellow, cyan and magenta

Color Printing

Newspapers usually print only in black and white, but a great many books and magazines print in full color. It would be impossible to print separately the thousands of different colors that exist, but fortunately all these colors can be reproduced on paper by combining together just three basic ink colors with black. They are yellow, magenta (red), and cyan (blue). So in color printing, four separate printing plates are used, which apply in turn yellow, magenta, cyan and black ink to the paper.

The separate printing plates are made from photographs taken of the original color picture through different colored filters. To get the yellow plate, a blue filter is used; to get magenta, a green filter; and to get cyan, a red filter.

Cyan

Black

Magenta and cyan

Yellow and cyan

The pictures on this page show how a color image is built up during color printing. The pictures at the top represent the four separate plates and the color they apply. The middle pictures show the colors created by combinations of the plates. The picture at the bottom left shows the three colors combined. That on the right shows the final picture, including black, which appears on the printed page.

Full color

Wrapping It Up

Most of the goods we buy are sold wrapped up in paper, cardboard, plastic or other materials. The wrapping, or packaging, helps protect the goods and keep them clean and fresh. This is particularly important for food, for example. Many goods are packaged attractively to help them sell. Many manufacturers spend a great deal of money on packaging for this reason.

Most mass-produced goods, such as candy, are packaged by automatic wrapping machines like those in the picture. Many of these machines can make three wrappings one after the other. For chocolate the inner wrapper may be "silver" foil. Next may come an intermediate wrapping of "see-through" cellophane, followed by an outer wrapping of printed paper. The wrappings are supplied from continu-

Supervisor

Manual unwrapper

ous reels and are then cut into individual sheets. These are then automatically folded around the goods and glued in position if need be.

The "silver" foil used for candy wrappings is not actually made of silver, but of aluminum. Cellophane is a transparent film made from woodpulp in much the same way as the man-made

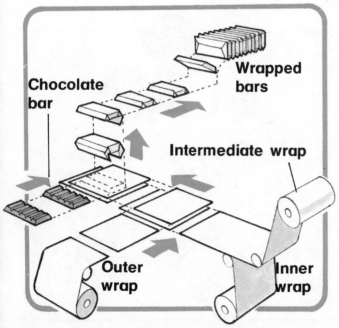

Chocolate bar

Wrapped bars

Intermediate wrap

Outer wrap

Inner wrap

fiber rayon. Another transparent film is also made from woodpulp – cellulose acetate. Ths is the same material that is used for photographic film.

Other film is made from plastics, such as polythene. Plastic film is also used to "shrink-wrap" goods. The film is placed over them and then a vacuum is applied to suck it down tightly on top. Plastic foams are also widely used for packaging fragile items, such as electrical equipment and cameras. The most widely used is light, white expanded polystyrene. This is shaped to keep fragile articles rigid inside an outer container.

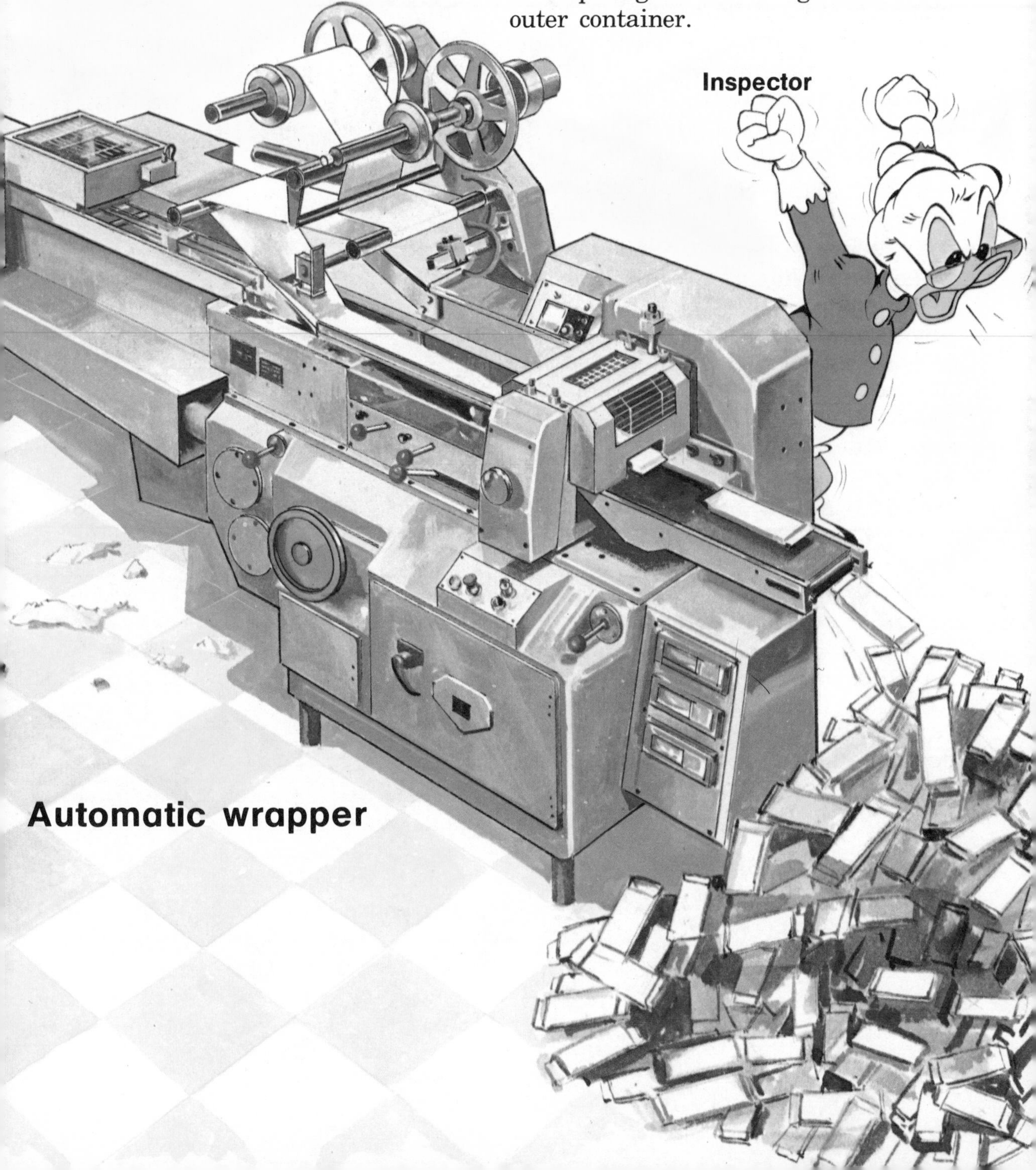

Inspector

Automatic wrapper

In the Can

Paper, cardboard and plastics are not good for packaging many kinds of food, such as fruit and vegetables. They are too easily punctured, which allows air and germs in and causes food to spoil. These foods have to be packaged in strong cans. Canning ia a big industry, which enables us to enjoy a very wide range of foods from all parts of the world all through the year.

The tin cans used for canning are not made only of tin. They are made from steel plate that has been coated with a thin layer of tin. The tin stops the steel beneath from rusting. The method of making tin cans is shown here. The tinplate is lacquered so that food juices and acids cannot attack it. The body blanks are cut out, formed into cylinders and then soldered. One end is attached by a double seaming process which makes the joint airtight.

The open cans are then fed into an automatic filling machine. This fills them with food that has been carefully trimmed and washed. The cans then go through an exhausting machine. One type of exhausting machine heats the filled cans to expel the air from them. Another type removes the air by suction. The cans are then automatically sealed.

The cans next have to be heated strongly to sterilize the food inside – that is, kill any germs or anything that may cause the food to spoil. Sterilization is usually done at high temperatures in giant pressure cookers. After cooling in water or air, the cans are labeled by machine and packed in boxes for shipment.

Canning

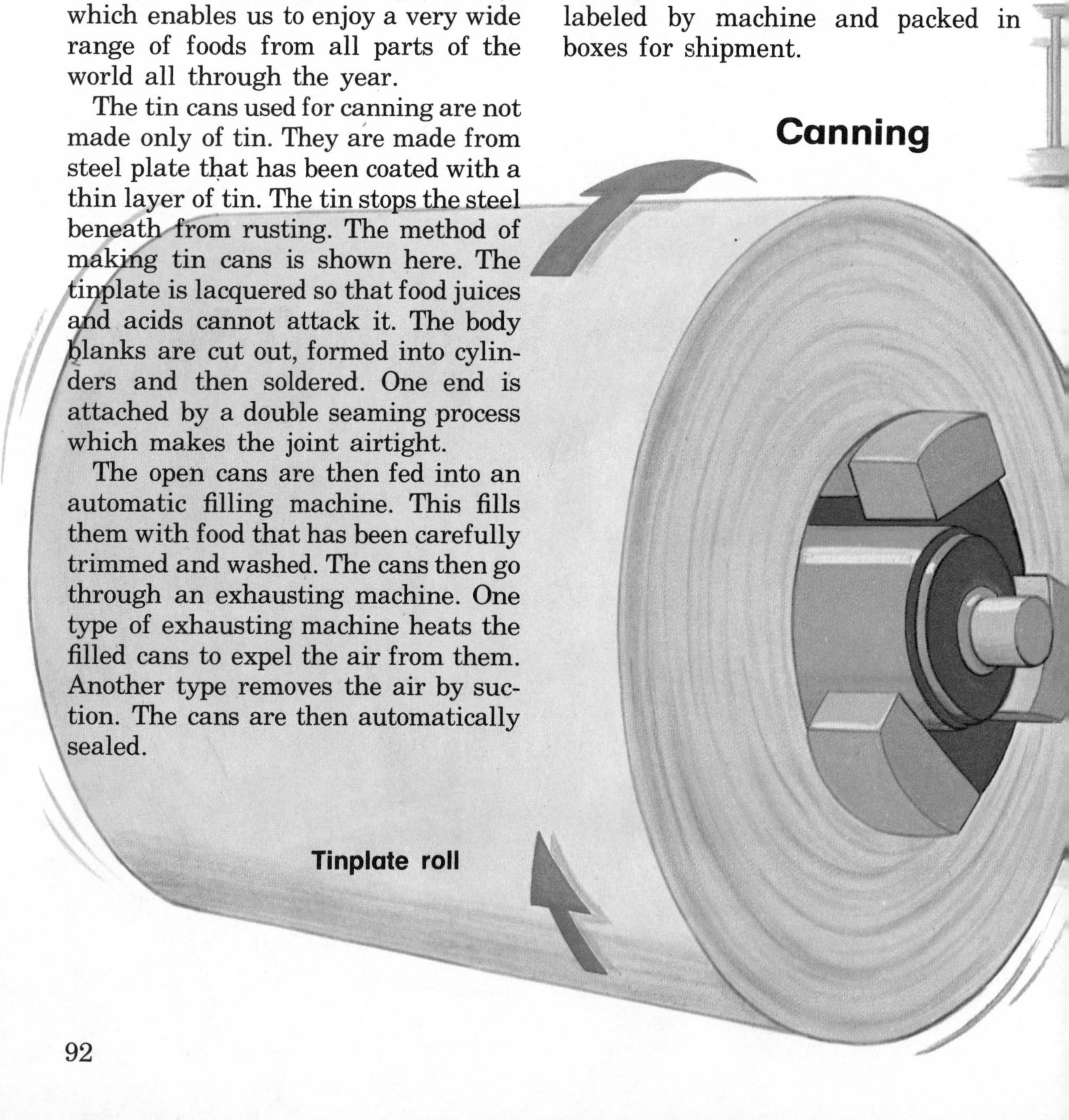

Tinplate roll

Making cans

Tinplate is lacquered

Body blanks are cut out

Blanks are made into cylinders

Can ends are punched out

Cylinder is soldered

Ends are attached and sealed by double sealing process

Can is tested under pressure

Some of the earliest objects made by men were containers such as pitchers, cooking pots and storage jars. They made these objects out of the clay they found in the ground. They would shape the objects in wet clay and then allow them to bake hard in the sun. Eventually they found how they could bake the clay in ovens, or kilns, to produce longer-lasting objects. They became potters.

Pottery made from clay is the most common of the products we call "ceramics." Ceramics also includes such things as cement, tiles, bricks and glass. All of these products are made from earthy materials that are baked or treated by fire in kilns or furnaces.

Ceramics

Jiggering and Jolleying

The majority of the ordinary pieces of pottery we are familiar with (plates, saucers, cups) are circular in shape or

Jigger

Shaper blade

Plate

Slip molding

Plaster mold

Shape to be cast

Slip poured in here

Water soaks into plaster

Clay layer forms

Clay slip

Two halves of mold

Slip molding

cross section. This is because of the way they are made. Traditionally, a potter makes all his wares using a potter's wheel. This is a revolving turntable on which he places a lump of wet clay. He then uses his fingers to shape the clay while it is rotating. This method of shaping is called throwing.

Hand throwing like this would be far too slow to make the quantities of tableware we need, so mechanical throwing processes are used, in which the potter uses simple machines. To make saucers and plates, for example, they use a machine called a jigger.

The jigger consists of a rotating mold, which shapes the upper surface of the plate. The potter places a "pancake" of wet clay on this mold and sets it turning. He then pulls down a handle

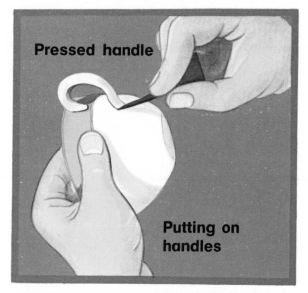

Pressed handle

Putting on handles

which lowers a shaped knife blade on to the clay. This shapes the bottom of the plate.

A similar kind of machine called a jolley is used to shape hollow objects like cups, for example. In this case, however, clay is forced into a hollow mold, and a knife blade is forced into it to shape the inside.

Other objects are shaped by different kinds of molding operations, particularly slip molding. "Slip" is liquid clay. In slip molding (casting) a hollow mold of the object you want is made in plaster in two halves. You fill the mold with slip and leave it for a while. The plaster gradually soaks up the water from the slip in contact with it, and a layer of clay forms. After a suitable time the remaining liquid slip is poured out, and the clay layer now lining the mold is allowed to dry. Then it can be removed by splitting open the mold.

Many objects, such as cup and jug handles, are made by pressing clay into molds. The handles are then attached to the cup or jug by means of liquid slip, which acts like glue.

Shaper blade

Mold

Jolleying

Firing and Finishing

After a piece of pottery has been shaped, it must be allowed to dry before it can be safely handled. When it is dry, it is stacked on carts and wheeled into the kiln for baking, or "firing." The kiln is a very hot oven, in which temperatures reach between 1,000° and 1,400°C.

The kiln is a chamber lined with refractory (heat-resistant) bricks and heated by burning gas or oil or by electricity. In the traditional kiln the clayware is stacked on shelves; the kiln is fired for a suitable time and then allowed to cool before being emptied. This is wasteful of both time and energy, so continuous kilns are now being used more and more. In these kilns the clayware is stacked and moved along, passing slowly along a tunnel that takes it through the firing zone. It emerges from the end of the tunnel cool enough to handle.

Low kiln temperatures are used for the cheaper kind of pottery, which is known as earthenware. High temperatures are used for the best kind of pottery—porcelain. At high temperatures the clay particles melt together to form a kind of glass. That is why real porcelain lets lights through and is watertight.

Ordinary earthenware on the other hand is dull and porous – it lets water through. To make it shiny and watertight, you have to glaze it. You dip it in a special liquid clay mixture called glaze and then fire it again. The glaze flows evenly over the surface of the pottery and forms a smooth glassy coating. Often glaze is applied after shaping and drying, and then there is only one firing.

The pottery may be decorated in a number of different ways, either before or after firing and glazing. It may be decorated with different colored slips and glazes. It may be decorated with molded figures, or formed into china figures. Patterns can also be applied to it by means of transfers or engraved designs. Some of the best pottery is hand-painted in enamel colors.

Glazing

Kiln

Fired
pottery

Hand
painting

Transfer printing

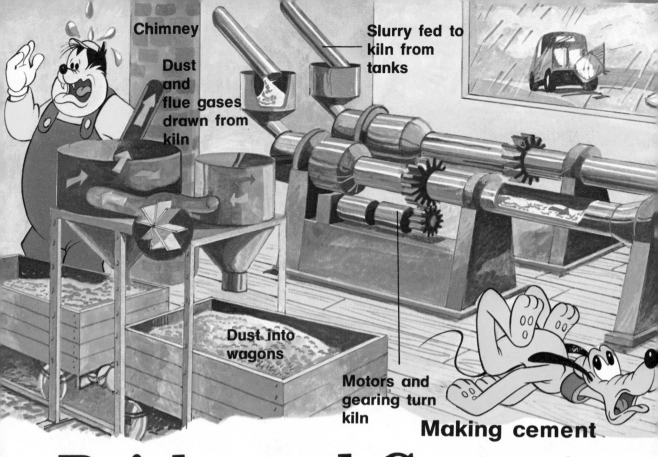

Chimney

Dust and flue gases drawn from kiln

Slurry fed to kiln from tanks

Dust into wagons

Motors and gearing turn kiln

Making cement

Bricks and Cement

Bricks have been an important building material for thousands of years. The earliest bricks were made of mud and straw and were baked in the sun. Houses made of mud bricks are still built in some parts of the world.

Elsewhere in the world, however, bricks are made from stronger materials and are baked, or "fired," in high-temperature kilns. Bricks are made from clays or from mixtures containing sand, lime and flint. First these materials are crushed. Then they are mixed together with water to form a stiff paste. After thorough pounding, the mixture is ready for shaping.

Most ordinary bricks are made by extrusion. A machine forces out a long ribbon of wet clay, which is cut up into bricks. Some bricks are molded. After the bricks have been shaped, they are allowed to dry before being placed in the kiln. Usually it is a tunnel kiln, with the firing zone in the middle. The bricks are stacked on cars that move slowly along the tunnel. They are in turn heated, fired and cooled.

Equally important as a building material is cement. When mixed with sand, gravel and water, it becomes concrete, which sets as hard as rock. When quite a lot of lime is added to the mixture, it is known as mortar. Mortar is used for joining bricks together when bricklaying.

Cement is made from such materials as clay, limestone, gypsum and iron ore. These materials are crushed fine

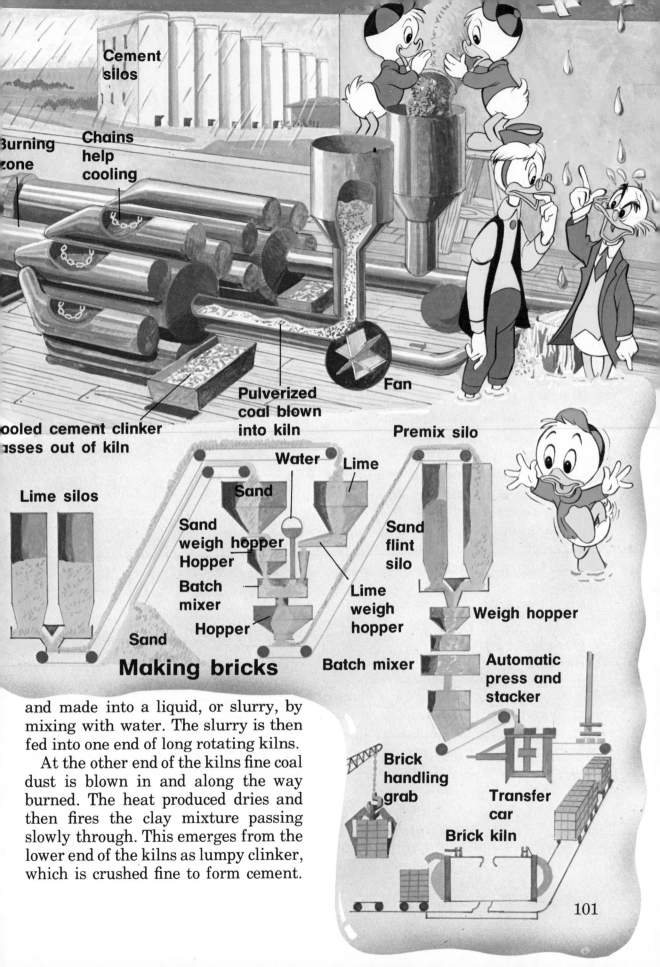

Cement silos

Burning zone

Chains help cooling

Cooled cement clinker passes out of kiln

Pulverized coal blown into kiln

Fan

Premix silo

Lime silos

Water

Lime

Sand

Sand weigh hopper
Hopper

Sand flint silo

Batch mixer

Hopper

Lime weigh hopper

Weigh hopper

Sand

Making bricks

Batch mixer

Automatic press and stacker

Brick handling grab

Transfer car

Brick kiln

and made into a liquid, or slurry, by mixing with water. The slurry is then fed into one end of long rotating kilns.

At the other end of the kilns fine coal dust is blown in and along the way burned. The heat produced dries and then fires the clay mixture passing slowly through. This emerges from the lower end of the kilns as lumpy clinker, which is crushed fine to form cement.

Making Glass

Glass is a remarkable material. It is easy to shape when hot and becomes transparent when it cools. It is hardly affected at all by other substances, which means that it can be used as a container for all kinds of foodstuffs and chemicals, and it is made from one of the cheapest materials there is—sand.

When making glass, a mixture of sand and limestone and soda ash is charged into a very hot furnace. There, the mixture melts into a red-hot liquid. Cullet, or waste glass is also usually added to make the mixture melt more easily. The molten glass is then shaped in a variety of ways to make the products we are familiar with.

To make ordinary window glass, a wide ribbon of molten glass is drawn vertically upward from the furnace. It gradually cools into a solid glass sheet, which is then cut to size. Because of the way in which it is drawn from the furnace, this sheet glass is not even or perfectly flat. A much better flat glass is made by the float process.

In the float-glass process, molten glass flows from the furnace on to the surface of a bath of molten tin. The surface of the tin is perfectly flat, and the glass flowing onto it becomes perfectly flat too. Overhead heaters help melt down any unevenness in the upper surface of the glass. The glass is then allowed to cool slowly in a cooling chamber, through which it passes on rollers.

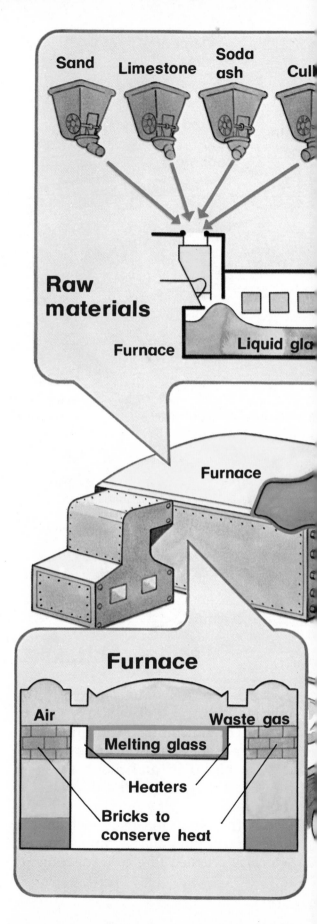

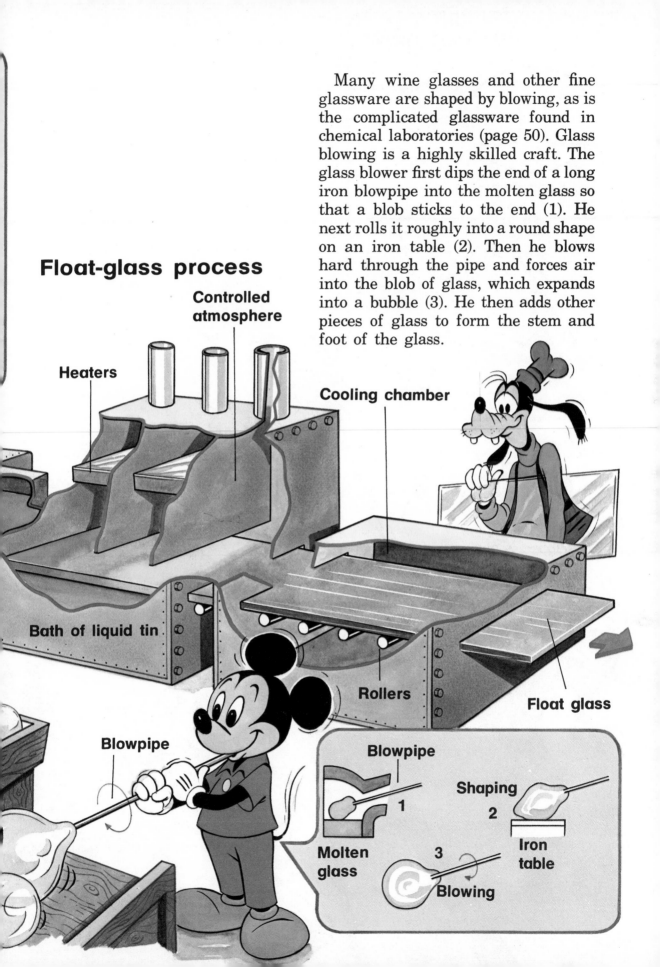

Many wine glasses and other fine glassware are shaped by blowing, as is the complicated glassware found in chemical laboratories (page 50). Glass blowing is a highly skilled craft. The glass blower first dips the end of a long iron blowpipe into the molten glass so that a blob sticks to the end (1). He next rolls it roughly into a round shape on an iron table (2). Then he blows hard through the pipe and forces air into the blob of glass, which expands into a bubble (3). He then adds other pieces of glass to form the stem and foot of the glass.

Float-glass process

Controlled atmosphere

Heaters

Cooling chamber

Bath of liquid tin

Rollers

Float glass

Blowpipe

Blowpipe

Shaping

2

Molten glass

1

3

Iron table

Blowing

Stained glass

Leaf or round

Core

Height or heart

Lead calme

Calme

Solder

Stained glass

The beauty of a fine piece of glassware can be increased by decorating it in a number of ways. One good way of doing this is by cutting. Glass is cut so that it sparkles when the light hits it. The best cut glassware is made from glass containing lead. Glass "cutting" is actually done by grinding the glass away with a rotating grinding wheel.

A smaller wheel made of copper is

Decorating Glass

Cut glass

Cutting wheel

Engraving

Spinning copper wheel

used to engrave glass with a delicate pattern. The spinning wheel scratches a design on the surface. Glass can be given a dull, or matte, surface by sandblasting – blowing sand against it.

Another method of decoration is etching. In this process a design is cut into the glass by means of a powerful acid called hydrofluoric acid. This is one of the very few chemicals that affects glass.

Glass can also be made more attractive by coloring it. It is easily colored by including certain metal minerals in the glassmaking recipe. For example, adding iron produces shades of green, cobalt produces blue, while copper produces red.

Fine works of art can be made by piecing together different colored bits of glass into what is called a stained glass window. The pieces are held in place by soft lead framing ("calme"), which is soldered together. The glass for stained glass windows is made deliberately full of air bubbles and uneven in thickness. It then varies in color and scatters the light in more interesting ways than if it were flat.

To make a window, an artist first draws a "cartoon," which shows in detail the shapes and colors to be used. After the pieces of glass have been made, he assembles them on his bench and draws in any further details with enamel paints. The pieces of glass are then "fired" slowly in a kiln to set the paint. Then they are put together in the lead framing to complete the window.

Beacon

Jungle drums

Broadcasting

GRANDE

We live in an age of excellent communications. By telephone we can talk to people in other cities and even other countries. On the radio and television we can hear and see things happening anywhere in the world.

Radio and television are the latest and best methods of sending information or signals over a distance. From early days men have devised means of sending long-distance messages. They would light beacons on hilltops as a prearranged signal to mean, for exam-

Old-fashioned radio set

Loudspeaker

Receiver

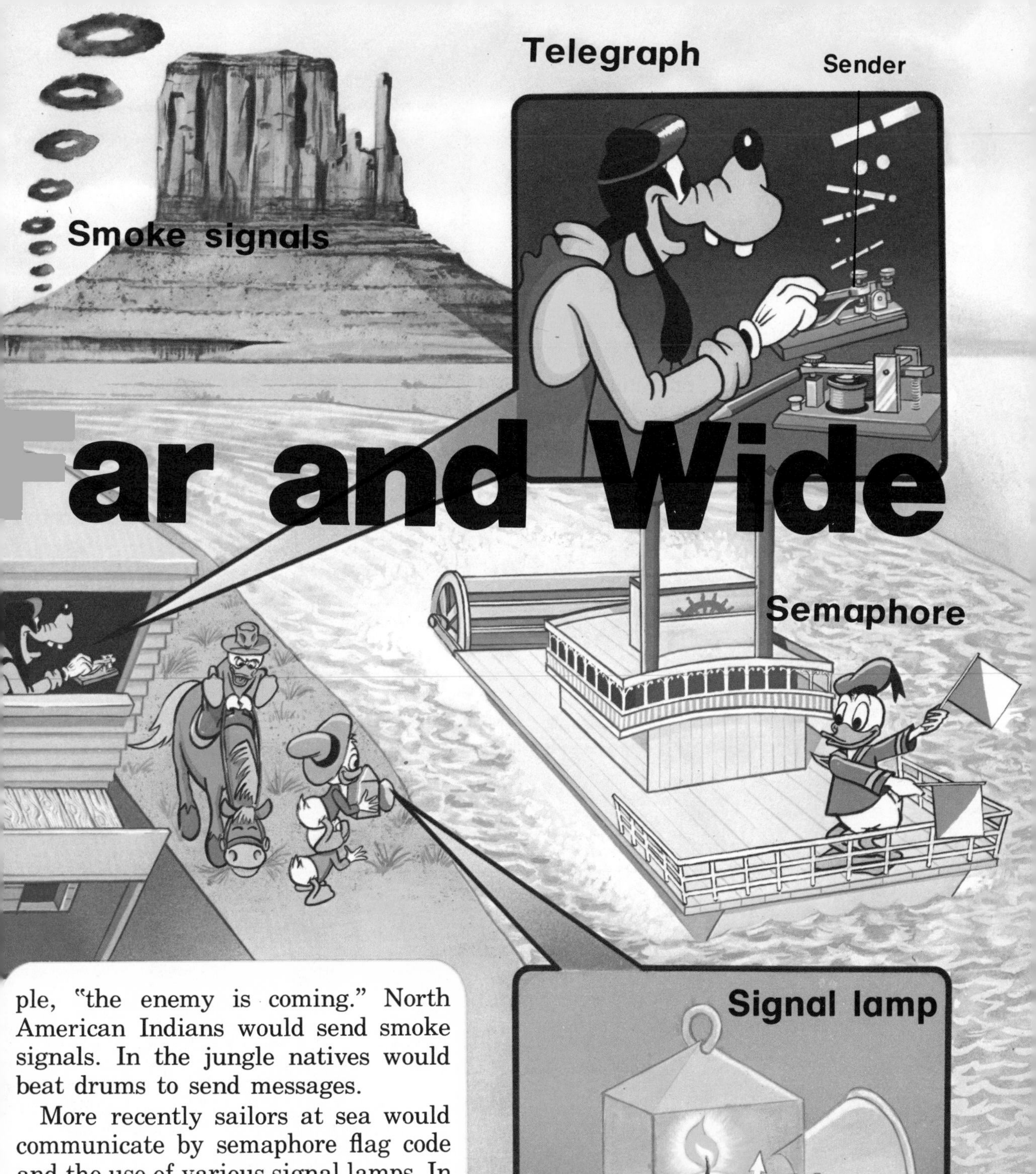

Sender

Smoke signals

Far and Wide

Semaphore

Signal lamp

ple, "the enemy is coming." North American Indians would send smoke signals. In the jungle natives would beat drums to send messages.

More recently sailors at sea would communicate by semaphore flag code and the use of various signal lamps. In semaphore, each letter of the alphabet is represented by the positions of two flags held in the hands. A signal lamp flashes messages in Morse Code, in which letters are represented by dots and dashes.

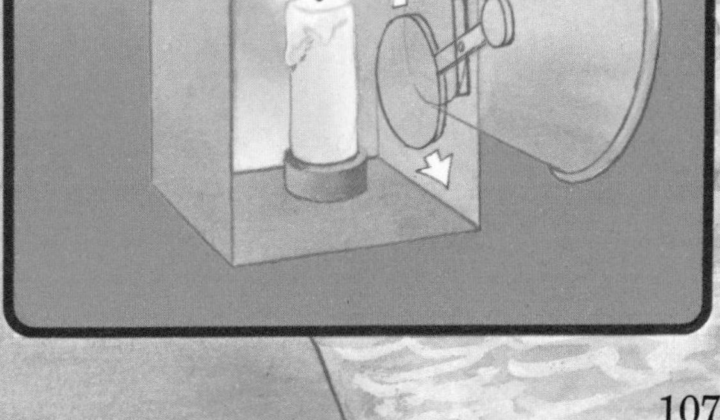

107

Here is the News

The picture shows what happens in a television studio while the news is being broadcast. One or more television cameras are directed on the newscaster, while a microphone is suspended above him on a long pole, or "boom." The boom is positioned so as to be just out of the picture.

TV camera

Electron gun

Lens

Electron beam

Electrical image

Camera operator

Viewfinder

TV camera

Camera dolly

Most newscasters only occasionally look down at their scripts, but they do not memorize what they have to say. They read it from a "Teleprompter" screen beneath the camera lens which shows the script in large letters.

Even a black-and-white TV camera works in a very complicated way. The camera lens focuses an image of the scene on to an electrically charged plate. This forms an electrical image of the scene. A beam of electrons from an electron gun then "scans" this image in a series of lines from left to right. Electrical signals coming from the scanning process vary according to the brightness of the original scene.

These signals are then transmitted and are picked up eventually by a TV receiver. This changes them back on the viewing screen into patterns of light and dark, which reproduce the original scene.

Color television is even more complicated. The camera has three electron guns, which record the brightness of three main colors (red, blue and green) in the scene viewed. The signals they produce are then transmitted and fed to the receiver screen, where they make red, blue and green colored dots glow. The colors merge together to form a colored reproduction of the original scene.

Microphone

Microphone boom

Newscaster

Script

Under Control

Even for newscasting there are usually two or three TV cameras which view the newscaster and anyone with him from different angles. In other studio productions there may be even more cameras. The pictures taken by the different cameras are not, of course, all shown at the same time. The director of the program selects whichever one he thinks is most suitable at any time.

He sits above the studio in a darkened control room. In front of him are TV "monitor" screens which show him the pictures being taken by the various cameras on the studio floor. By pressing a switch he selects one of the camera views for broadcasting, and this appears on another screen called the transmission monitor. A red light appears on the camera which has been selected.

In practice, for many programs, the positions of the cameras, the views they will take, and the order in which they will be switched in is worked out in advance. Detailed instructions for the cameras and control room staff are written down on the camera script. The director sits in the control room and directs the camera crews by microphone. He usually has someone called the vision mixer on hand to switch over from camera to camera.

TV camer

Videotape monitor screen

Clock

Camera
monitor
screen

Transmission
monitor
screen

Selector
switches

111

Special Effects

In both television and films directors often use tricks, or "special effects" to fool the viewers. For example, they can make people disappear like magic.

One quite simple method used is back projection. A scene is projected on which shows the horse and rider apparently traveling over the prairie.

Further special effects can be obtained by speeding up or slowing down the rate at which the camera shoots the film. Ordinarily a movie cam-

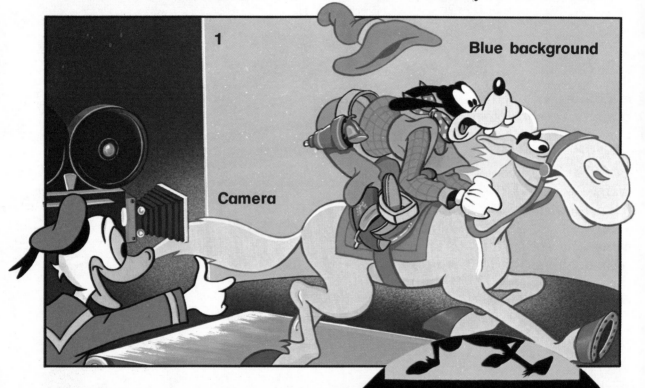

a translucent screen behind the actors to form a background to the action taking place.

A more realistic effect is obtained by the use of a traveling matte. First the horse and rider are filmed in the studio against a blue background (1). Then a copy of the film is made which has the horse and rider masked out (2). Using the mask, the background of the scene is filmed on the prairie, getting a result like (3). This is then combined with film (1) to produce the final film (4),

Traveling matte

3 Background with traveling matte

in the studio can be whisked to far-away places. In the studio, he appears before a camera against a blue background. The camera sends signals into a "mixer" unit which also receives signals representing the distant scene.

In the mixer is a switching unit which can switch from one set of signals to the other in an instant. Where the camera sees the blue background, the distant scene is transmitted, and where the camera sees the reporter, his picture is transmitted.

era takes 24 pictures, or frames, a second. To show faster than normal movement, the camera is slowed down to only 12 frames a second. Then, when the film is projected at the usual 24 frames a second, the action appears to happen twice as fast. Similarly, when you want to show slow motion, the camera is speeded up to 36 frames a second. When the film is projected at the normal speed, the action appears slowed down.

In television, two or more pictures can be combined together to give interesting effects. For example, a reporter

4 Combination

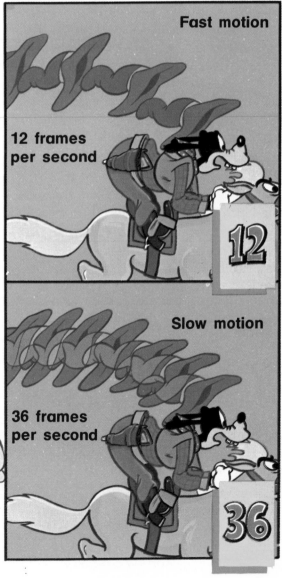

Fast motion

12 frames per second

12

Slow motion

36 frames per second

36

113

Cartoon Time

The cartoons that we all enjoy look as if they are simple to make, but in fact making cartoons is quite a complicated process and takes a long time. Thousands of separate drawings have to be made even for a short film.

An ordinary film consists of a series of still pictures, or "frames." Each frame shows anything moving in a slightly different position from the frame before. When the frames are projected on a screen one after the other, things appear to move.

To make cartoons, a series of drawings are produced, showing anything moving in slightly different positions. These drawings are then photographed and become the frames of the film. When they are projected, characters in them appear to move. This technique is called animation.

The pictures here show how a cartoon is made. First a writer thinks up a story and writes a script (1). This describes the plot and the action and sets down what the characters will say. Next a series of rough sketches is drawn which show the story rather like a strip cartoon (2). This stage is called the storybook.

While the story is being worked out in detail, an artist is sketching out ideas for the main characters and the background for the action (3). These will then guide the artists who prepare the finished drawings (4, 5, 6).

The moving characters are usually drawn on clear celluloid sheets ("cels"), which are then positioned over the background and photographed with it.

The drawings are laid flat on a table and photographed by a camera mounted vertically above (7). The finished filmstrip is shown in picture 8.

The finished film

7

Photo-graphing the drawings

114

115

Men have been sailing the seven seas for at least 5,000 years. Until about 200 years ago all ships had sails and were powered by the wind. Now they are powered by steam turbines or diesel engines, and are propelled by propellers, or "screws."

As you can see from the picture, ships come in all shapes and sizes! Some of the smallest are local fishing boats, which fish just offshore. The biggest are passenger-carrying liners and oil tankers, which may be more than 1,000 feet (300 meters) long. A fascinating variety of other craft can also be found at sea, from tugs and car ferries to hovercraft and submarines. Each of these ships plays its part in making shipping one of the world's greatest industries.

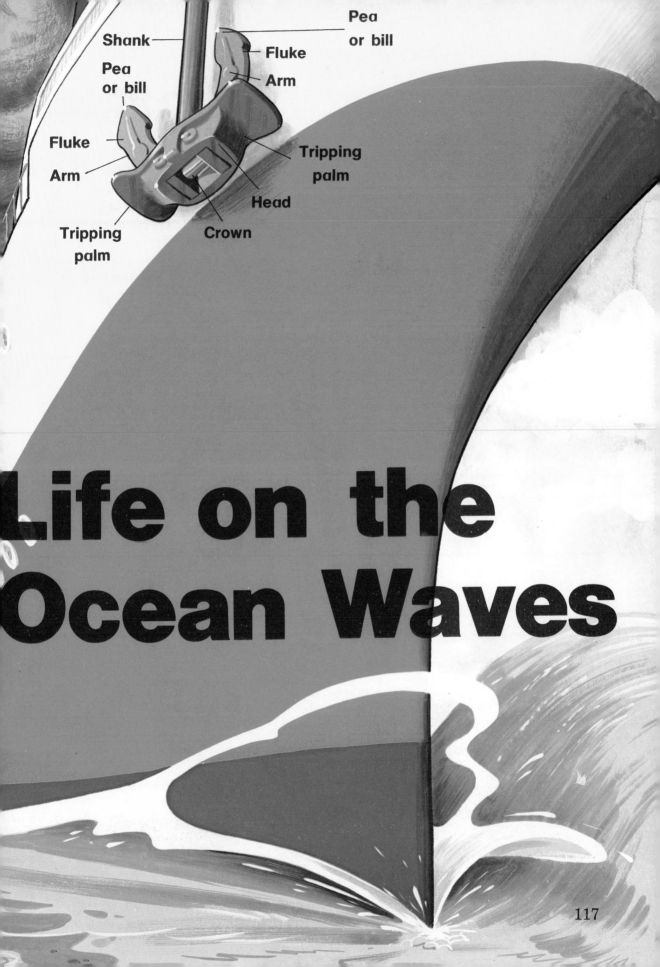

Shank

Pea or bill

Fluke

Arm

Pea or bill

Fluke

Arm

Tripping palm

Tripping palm

Head

Crown

Life on the Ocean Waves

In Port

The best place to see different types of ships is at a port or harbor.

The picture shows a typical harbor scene. A tough and powerful tug is maneuvering a huge ocean liner inside the narrow waterway. If the currents and tide are tricky, a team of tugs may be needed. The tugs tow the liners with tow ropes and also push them with padded bows (front).

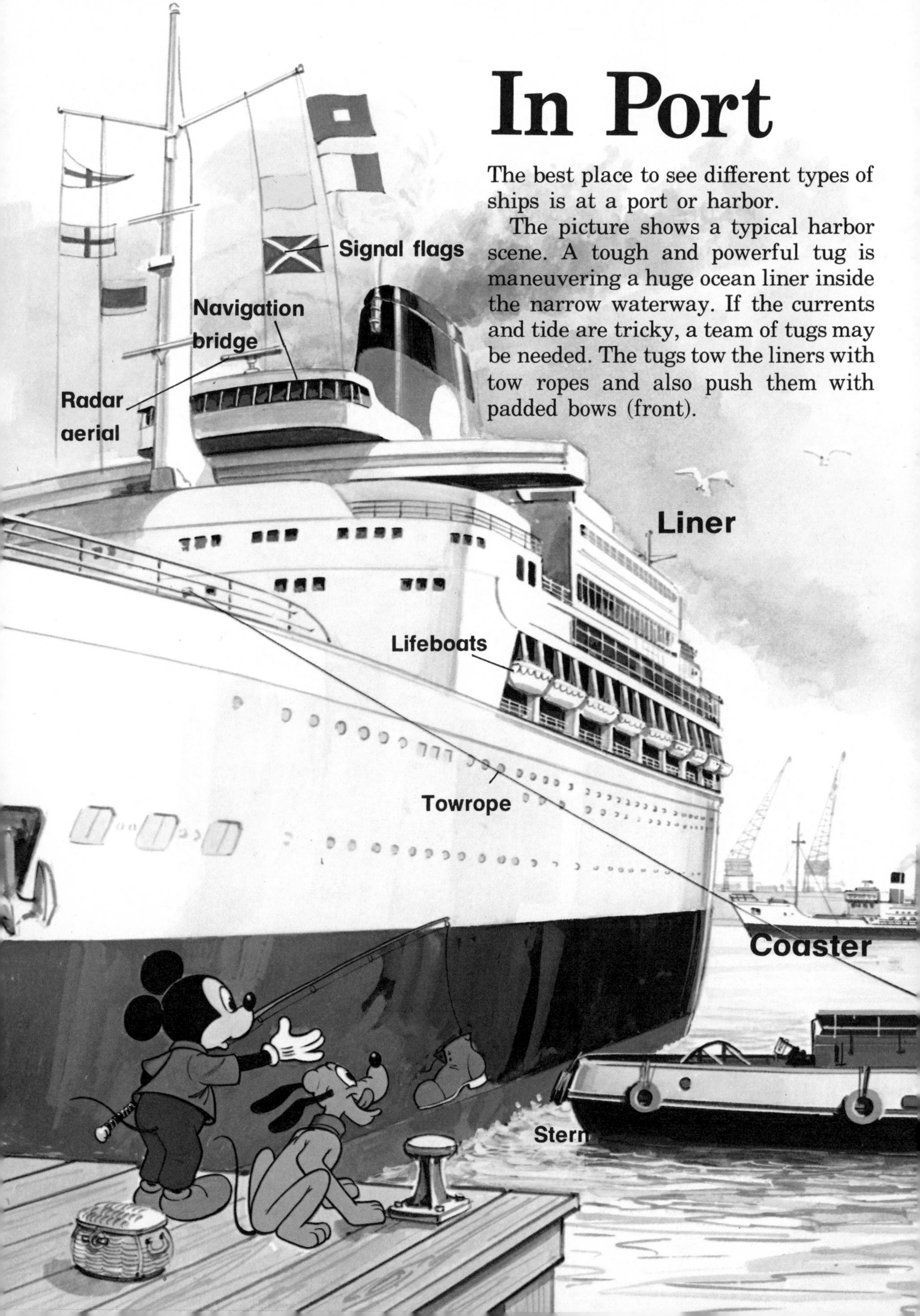

Signal flags

Navigation bridge

Radar aerial

Liner

Lifeboats

Towrope

Coaster

Stern

The small ship, or cargo ship in the background carries general goods from port to port, traveling when and where there is cargo to be carried. Such ships usually have quite a shallow draft so that they can navigate in shallow river channels and estuaries. The other vessel shown here seldom goes to sea. It is a dredger, which moves along the navigation channels leading into the harbor. Its job is to keep the channels deep enough for shipping. It dredges, or digs out, the mud and sand that the ocean and river currents and the tides bring in. It digs by means of a series of buckets that circulate on an endless chain. The bucket chain angles down through the water to the seabed, removing mud and sand continuously. The dredger deposits the dredged material in a hopper, or barge, moored alongside.

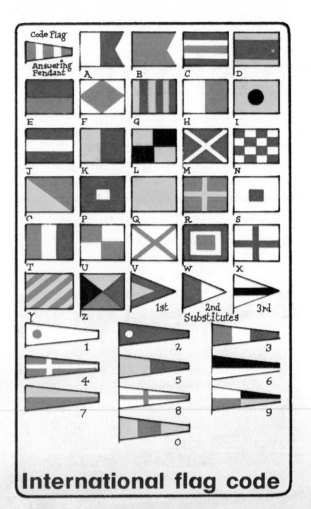

International flag code

Harbor lights

Bridge

Bucket dredger

Barge

Bow

Tug

nch

Fishing Boats

When you go fishing in the river, you use a rod and line to catch fish. Fishermen may also go line fishing at sea fairly close inshore. They use a long line with many short lines and hooks attached to it. They bait the hooks and throw the line overboard.

The inshore fisherman may also set traps for crabs and lobsters, with the so-called "inkpot" lobster pots. The lobsters or crabs can easily get in through the top opening, but find it difficult to get out.

Offshore fishermen most often use nets to fish. The drifter is a small boat which usually has a small sail to steady her while she is drifting. (Ships are always called "she.") The drift net is very long and hangs vertically in the water from floats. The fish try to swim through it and get caught by their gills if they are large enough.

The trawler is usually a much stur-

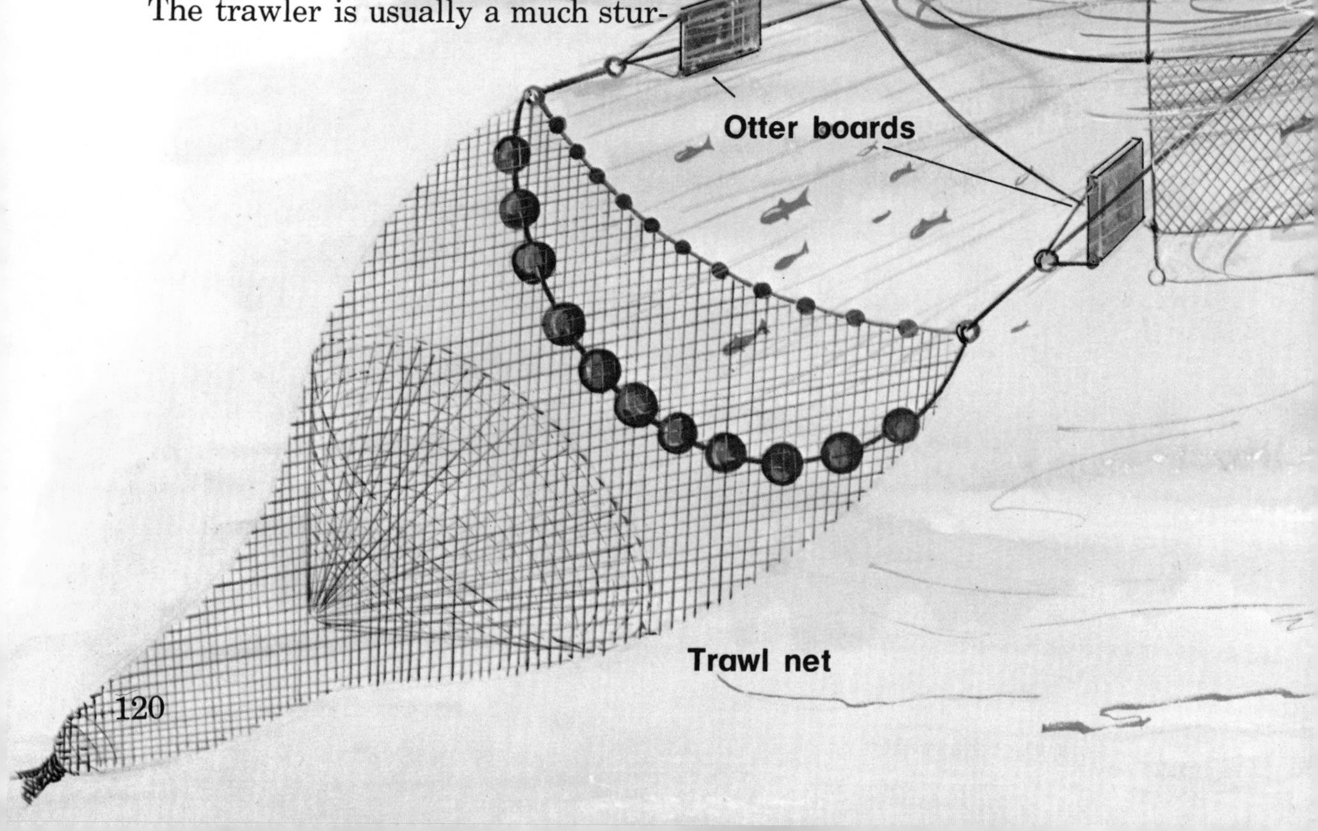

Sail

Drifter

Otter boards

Trawl net

120

Stern trawler

dier boat with a powerful winch. It catches fish by dragging a bag-shaped net either along the bottom or at any depth below the surface. The mouth of the trawl net is kept open by means of two boards ("otter" boards) or by a beam.

Another common sea fishing method is seining. A large net is cast into the sea around a shoal of fish. The ends of the net are brought together, trapping the fish inside. Of course, you have got to find your shoal first! But, like most fishing boats these days, seiners have sonar or echo-sounding instruments to help them find the shoals of fish.

Warps

Floats

Drift net

Inshore fisherman

Float

Opening

Inkpot type crab and lobster pot

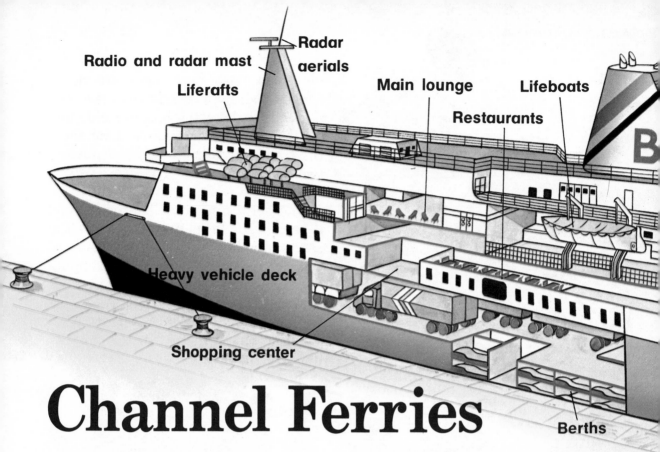

Radio and radar mast

Radar aerials

Liferafts

Main lounge

Lifeboats

Restaurants

Heavy vehicle deck

Shopping center

Berths

Channel Ferries

A special kind of ship is used on short sea crossings like the English Channel in Europe. These Channel "ferries" carry passengers and often their vehicles back and forth all through the year and in all but the stormiest weather. They are fine examples of modern ships, designed with the comfort of passengers very much in mind.

The ferry pictured here looks much like a passenger liner. It has a large superstructure – that is the part above the main deck. It has lounges, restaurants and bars, together with a shopping center. There is plenty of deck space for sunning yourself. Lifeboats and liferafts are at hand ready for immediate use in emergencies. There are also numerous cabins with berths (beds) for overnight sleeping accommodation.

However, a large proportion of the "below-decks" area is taken up with parking space for passengers' cars and, on this ferry, even buses and trucks. Some ferries also have railroad decks so they can carry railroad cars. Railroad cars are shunted on at one port and are hauled off at the other to continue their journey.

In this particular ferry the vehicles are loaded and unloaded by a ramp at the stern, but there are other loading arrangements. Some ferries have a bow (front) ramp as well; others have a side ramp.

Ferries have to be extremely easy to maneuver, since they travel into and out of port several times a day. They usually have twin propellers at the stern and also small propellers ("thrusters") at the sides or the bow.

Modern ferries are well prepared for rough weather as they are fitted with stabilizers. These are large fins that project from the sides of the hull beneath the waterline. They are controlled by gyroscopes. In heavy seas a ship tends to roll, or move from side to side, which is very unpleasant for the passengers. Stabilizers work by pushing against the water in such a way that the ship cannot roll very much.

Sundecks

Upper car deck

Lower car deck

Loading ramps

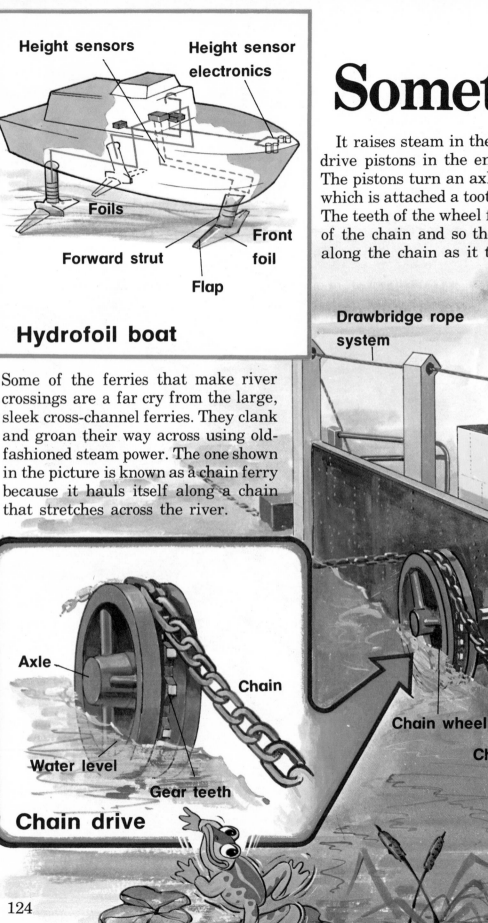

Hydrofoil boat

Height sensors

Height sensor electronics

Foils

Forward strut

Front foil

Flap

Something

It raises steam in the boilerhouse to drive pistons in the engine cylinders. The pistons turn an axle, to the end of which is attached a toothed gearwheel. The teeth of the wheel fit into the links of the chain and so the wheel travels along the chain as it turns. A simple

Drawbridge rope system

Axle

Pistons

Some of the ferries that make river crossings are a far cry from the large, sleek cross-channel ferries. They clank and groan their way across using old-fashioned steam power. The one shown in the picture is known as a chain ferry because it hauls itself along a chain that stretches across the river.

Chain wheel

Chain

Chain drive

Axle

Chain

Water level

Gear teeth

Old, Something New

hand-operated drawbridge is lowered at either end to allow passengers and vehicles on and off.

In complete contrast is another type of boat now coming into ferry service on many river, harbor and short sea crossings. It is the hydrofoil boat. This boat is fitted with what are really underwater wings ("foils").

The foils are attached by struts to the boat's hull, and when the boat is traveling fast they start to lift, just as a plane's wing lifts when it travels fast through the air (see page 64). The lift of the foils raises the boat's hull clear of the water. When its hull is out of the water, the boat is no longer slowed down by water resistance. Because of this it can travel at very high speeds — over 70 mph (110 km/h).

Boiler house

Boiler

Drawbridge

125

Flying Boats

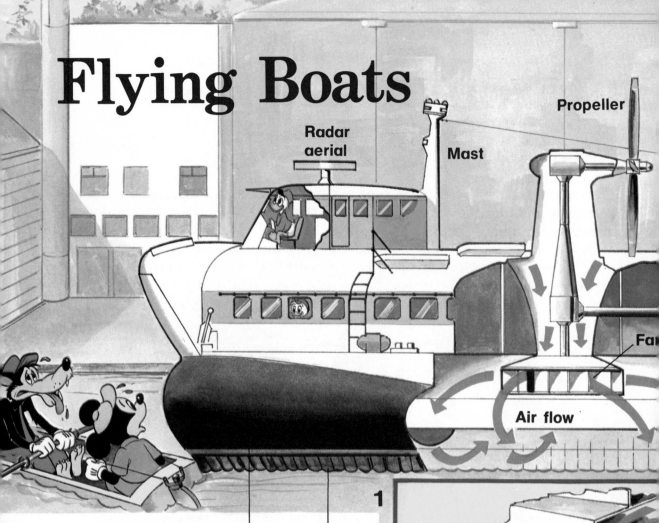

Radar aerial

Mast

Propeller

Fan

Air flow

1

Skirt　　**Fingers**

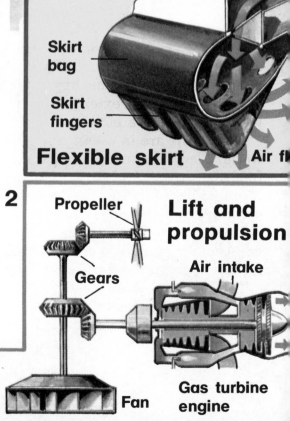

Skirt bag

Skirt fingers

Flexible skirt

Air fl

2

Propeller

Gears

Lift and propulsion

Air intake

Fan

Gas turbine engine

The hydrofoil boat (page 124) is one of the fastest craft on water, but not the fastest. Faster still is the hovercraft, which is also called an air-cushion vehicle (ACV). The hovercraft does not travel in or on the water but just above it. Thus it is completely free from any water resistance and can therefore travel very fast – up to 95 mph (150 km/h).

The hovercraft glides above the water (or land for that matter) on a "cushion" of air. The cushion is produced by blowing air underneath the craft with powerful fans. To stop the

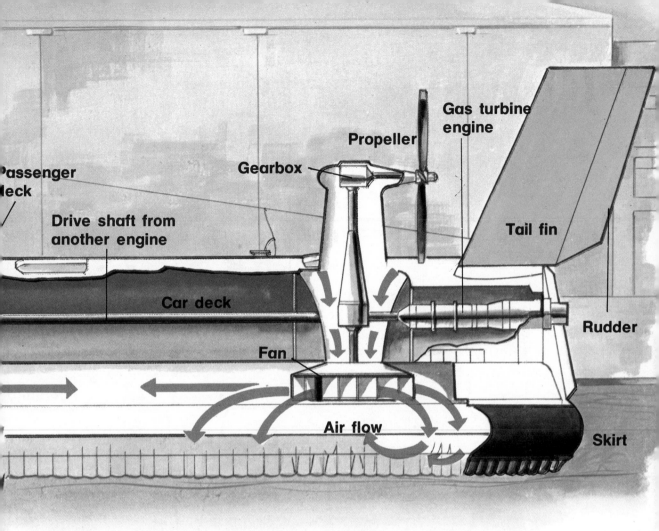

Passenger deck

Drive shaft from another engine

Gearbox

Propeller

Gas turbine engine

Tail fin

Car deck

Fan

Rudder

Air flow

Skirt

air leaking away too fast, the hovercraft has a "skirt" around the lower edge. This takes the form of a kind of bulbous tire with flexible fingers at the bottom. The fingers extend down to the water surface (see box 1).

Hovercraft are in use all around the world. They are used by the armed forces as troop carriers, gunships and reconnaissance craft, particularly in swampy coastal regions where wheeled vehicles and ordinary boats could not go. Another major use of hovercraft is for ferry service on short sea passages.

The largest and most successful hovercraft—the SRN4—is used as a passenger-car ferry across the English Channel. The "stretched" version of the SRN4 is 185 feet (56 meters) and 92 feet (28 meters) across. It can carry over 400 passengers and over 50 cars.

The general design of the SRN4 is shown above. Power is provided by four gas turbine engines located at the rear. These engines each drive a fan to give lift, and also a propeller to give thrust to propel the craft (box 2). They drive the propellers through an arrangement of shafts and gears. The propellers face backward and push the craft along. (In propeller-driven planes, the propellers "pull.") The hovercraft is steered by means of rudders on the twin tail fins at the rear. These work in the same way as a plane's rudder, deflecting the airstream so that the craft turns.

Finding your Way at Sea

Finding your way on the oceans is not an easy task. When you are out of sight of land, there are no recognizable points to refer to – just flat water

Sextant

Half plain glass

Index glass

Telescope

Half mirror

Index bar

Scale

Horizon glass

Arc

Reading

Micrometer

Buoy

WRECK

Taking a "fix"

Skipper

all around. Only when you get nearer the shore do things get easier, for you may be able to recognize landmarks.

Finding your way at sea is known as navigating. One of the most important things you must have to help you navigate is a chart. This is a detailed map that shows such things as the coastline, sandbanks, dangerous rocks and the position of buoys and lighthouses.

In addition to a chart, you need certain instruments to help you navigate. A vital one is a compass. This shows you the direction in which you are traveling. Another one is an echo-sounder. This is an instrument which tells you how deep the water is beneath the boat. It works by means of sound waves. It sends out sound waves, which are reflected back to it from the seabed. The time it takes for the sound "echoes" to return is a measure of the depth of water.

If you are voyaging out of sight of land for long periods, you will need a sextant with which you measure the angle of heavenly bodies above the horizon. This angle depends on the time and on your latitude. By noting the time and measuring the angle of, say, the sun, you can find out from navigation tables where you are.

To take a sextant "fix" (sighting), you look through the telescope and the clear half of the horizon glass at the horizon. Then you move the index bar until an image of the sun appears in the horizon glass to touch the horizon. You read the angle from the scale.

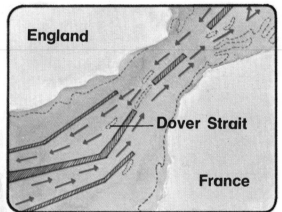

England

Dover Strait

France

Shipping lanes

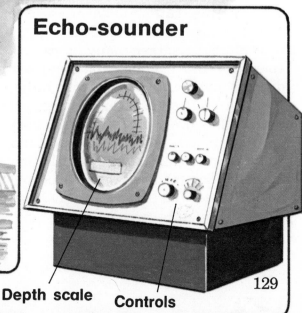

Echo-sounder

Crew

Depth scale   Controls

129

On the Rocks

Among the worst hazards at sea are jagged offshore rocks, which can rip open the hull of even the strongest ships. In heavy seas the rocks may be invisible until it is too late to avoid them. Often, therefore, these rocks have lighthouses built on them.

Lighthouses are usually tall towers made of stone, concrete or steel. They stand out above the rocks by day, and by night flash a warning light. Near hazards such as sandbanks where a lighthouse cannot be built, a lightship is moored instead. The ship has a light tower similar to a lighthouse.

At the top of a lighthouse is the lantern room, which contains the light-making apparatus. In the past most lighthouses had gas lamps, using acetylene gas which burns with a brilliant flame. Many lighthouses now have electric lamps. The lamp is surrounded by a lens system, which concentrates the light into a powerful beam. The lens system often rotates so that the lighthouse gives out a flashing light. Every lighthouse gives out a different pattern of flashes so that it can be easily recognized at night.

In stormy weather many ships and boats get into trouble and send out distress signals. If they have a radio, they transmit a "Mayday" emergency call, or they fire a distress rocket from a rocket pistol. Then other ships and shore rescue teams spring into action. Often lifeboatmen are the first people on the scene. The lifeboat they use has powerful engines and is very stable and buoyant. This means that it is difficult to capsize (overturn) or sink. In many countries lifeboatmen remain on call for lifeboat duty whenever they are not at sea themselves.

The Coast Guard may also become involved. They may send in helicopters to take off the crew of the wallowing vessel. If the vessel wrecks itself on rocks near the shore, the Coast Guard may rescue the crew in a "breeches buoy." This is a harness that slides along a line attached to the ship.

Lifejacket

Lifeboat

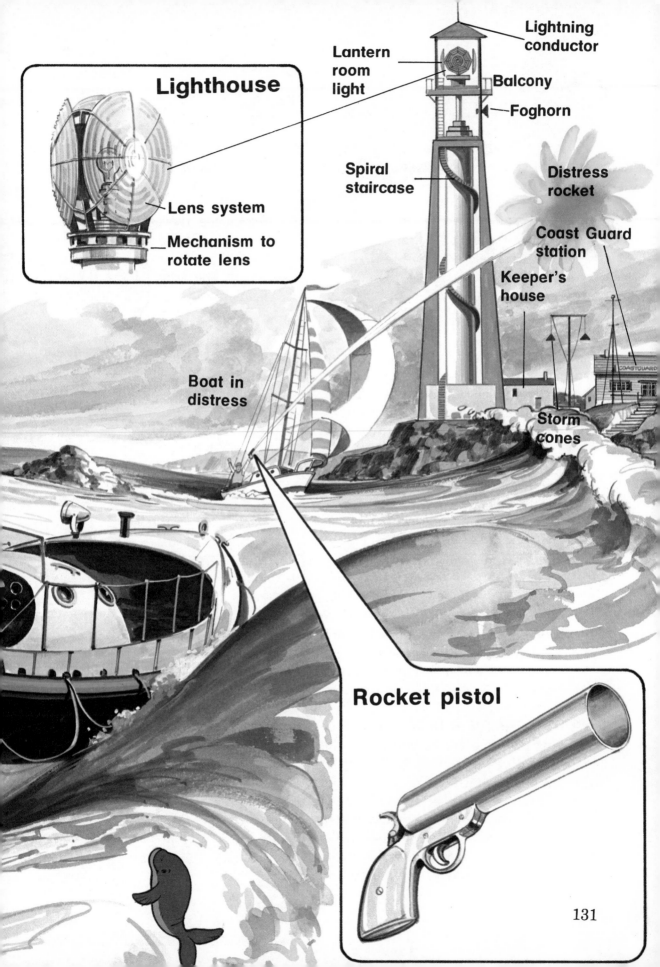

Lighthouse

Lens system

Mechanism to rotate lens

Lantern room light

Lightning conductor

Balcony

Foghorn

Spiral staircase

Distress rocket

Coast Guard station

Keeper's house

Storm cones

Boat in distress

Rocket pistol

131

Propeller

Upper rudder

Aft escape hatch

Nuclear reactor

Starboard diving plane

Engine rooms

Beneath the Waves

Some of the most fascinating craft at sea are those designed to travel under the water rather than on the surface. These are submarines used mainly by the navy. They have the advantage over surface ships in that they can disappear from view in a few minutes, making them difficult to locate. The latest nuclear-powered submarines can even remain under water for months at a time if need be!

A submarine can dive to different depths and then surface again simply by adjusting its weight. It does this by means of its ballast tanks. These are tanks at the sides of the vessel which can be filled with water or emptied. The amount of water left in the tanks determines how deep the submarine goes.

The box at the bottom of the page explains how the tanks work. On the surface, valves or vents, at the top of the tanks are shut (1). To descend, the vents are opened, allowing air to escape (2). At the same time water flows into the bottom of the tanks through the free flood holes. When the vessel has descended far enough (3),

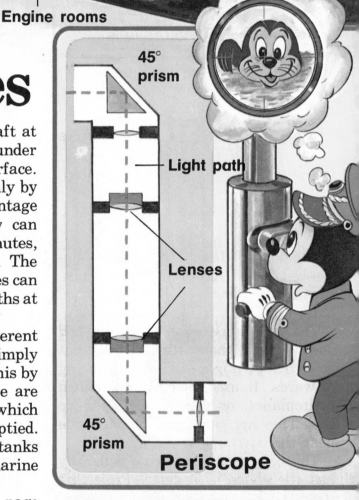

45° prism

Light path

Lenses

45° prism

Periscope

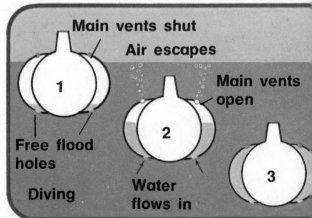

Main vents shut

Air escapes

Main vents open

1

2

3

Free flood holes

Diving

Water flows in

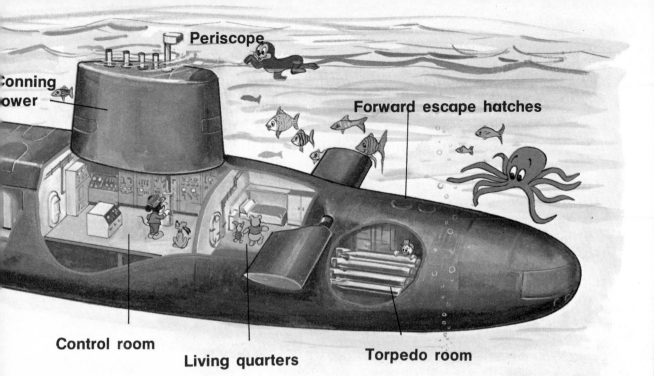

Periscope

Conning tower

Forward escape hatches

Control room

Living quarters

Torpedo room

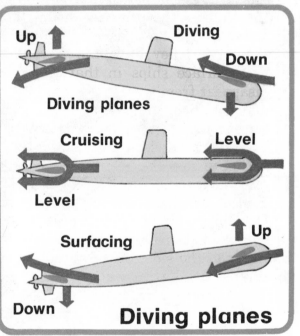

Up — Diving — Down

Diving planes

Cruising — Level

Level

Surfacing — Up

Down — **Diving planes**

the vents are closed. To surface, compressed air is forced into the tanks, expelling water through the free flood holes (4 and 5).

The submarine does not go up and down through the water vertically, but does so at an angle while it is traveling forwards. It uses movable fins called hydroplanes, or diving planes, to do this. They are positioned on each side near the bow and at the stern.

The body of a submarine generally has the shape of a cigar. Projecting

from it is a conning tower, or "sail." This acts as a navigation bridge when the submarine is traveling on the surface. Coming out of the conning tower is a periscope. This can be extended up to the surface while the submarine is still submerged, enabling the captain to see without being seen.

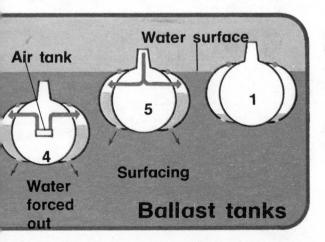

Air tank

Water surface

5

1

4

Surfacing

Water forced out

Ballast tanks

133

Exploring the Depths

Oceans cover nearly three-quarters of the Earth's surface, but only recently have men begun to explore and work in the ocean depths on a large scale. Scientists explore the oceans to search for valuable minerals. Engineers work on the seabed laying pipelines and construction oil rigs. They can do quite a lot in diving suits, but they also need underwater craft to help them.

Ordinary military submarines are designed purely as fighting vessels. They are not good for other underwater activities. So, much smaller mini-submarines called submersibles have been built. They are fitted with view-

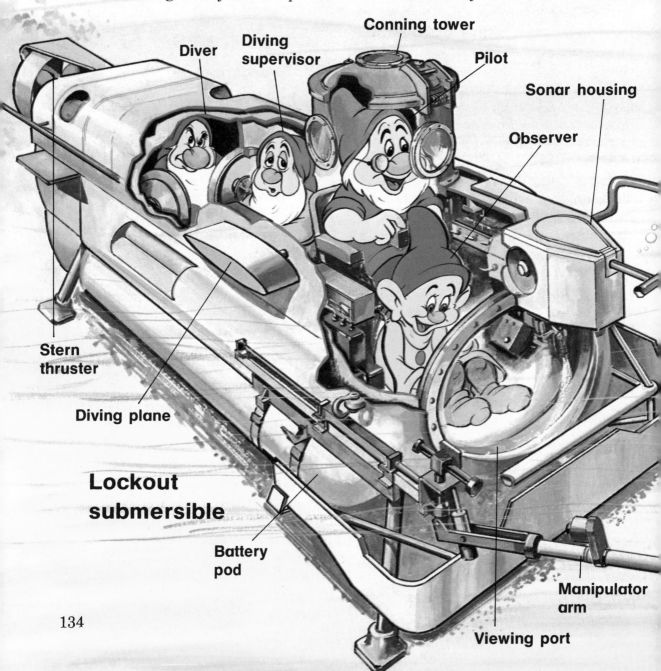

Diver

Diving supervisor

Conning tower

Pilot

Sonar housing

Observer

Stern thruster

Diving plane

Lockout submersible

Battery pod

Manipulator arm

Viewing port

134

ing ports for observation, floodlights, cameras and closed-circuit television. They have powered, jointed manipulator arms that can handle tools. They have radios so that they can communicate with surface ships and divers. They use sonar equipment to help them navigate. This equipment sends out sound signals and picks up the echoes from objects in their path.

The latest type of submersible is the lockout submersible pictured here. It has two separate compartments. In front is the crew compartment for the pilot and observer. Behind is the diving compartment. This has a hatch that can be opened under water to allow divers to leave or enter. It can be pressurized to whatever is the pressure of the water outside.

Divers use the lockout submersible to ferry them down to their place of work on the seabed. Afterwards they return, still under pressure, to their support ship, where they also live under pressure. Living in this way,

they do not have to spend a long time every day returning slowly to ordinary atmospheric pressure. Slow depressurization is necessary after diving to prevent the diver getting "the bends." This is a very painful condition caused by bubbles of gas forming inside the blood vessels of the body.

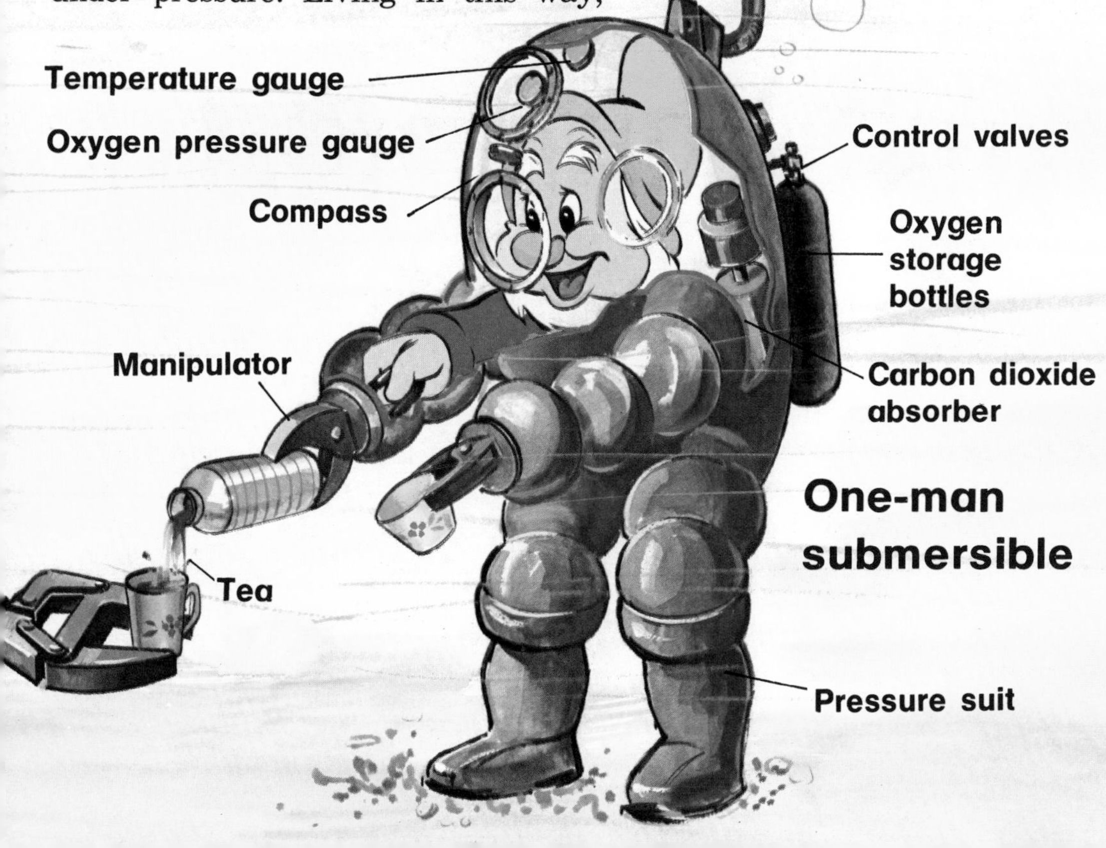

Lifting cable and telephone links

Temperature gauge

Oxygen pressure gauge

Compass

Control valves

Oxygen storage bottles

Manipulator

Carbon dioxide absorber

Tea

One-man submersible

Pressure suit

135

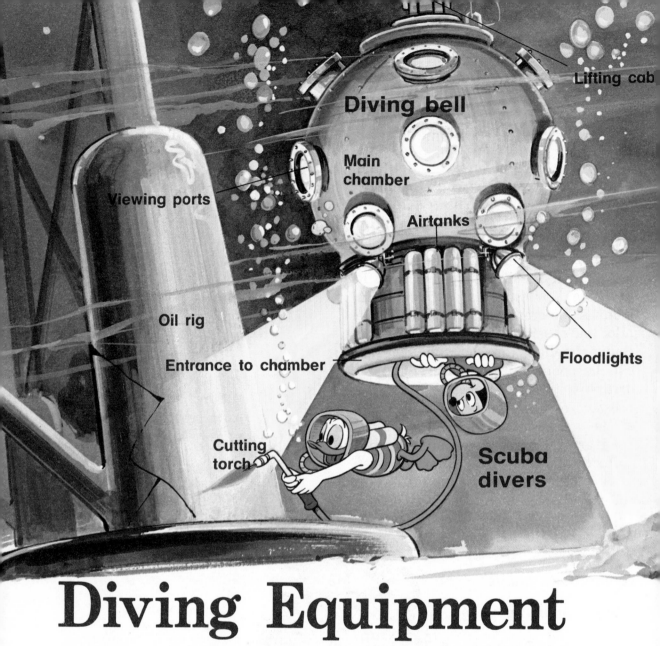

Lifting cab

Diving bell

Main chamber

Airtanks

Viewing ports

Oil rig

Entrance to chamber

Floodlights

Cutting torch

Scuba divers

Diving Equipment

Fish can breathe in water because they can remove oxygen from it with their gills. Since human divers do not have gills, they have to carry a supply of oxygen when they venture into the ocean depths. The most convenient method of doing so is to use scuba equipment. Scuba stands for "Self-Contained Underwater Breathing Apparatus."

The diver has strapped on his back one or two tanks containing compressed air or oxygen. A hose connects the tanks to the face mask through a system of valves. When he breathes out, his breath escapes into the water as bubbles. This kind of breathing apparatus is known as an aqualung.

To enable him to stay under water more easily, the scuba diver wears a heavy leaded belt. To swim more easily he wears swim fins, or flippers, which are shaped like duck feet. If he is going to dive for long in cold water, he wears

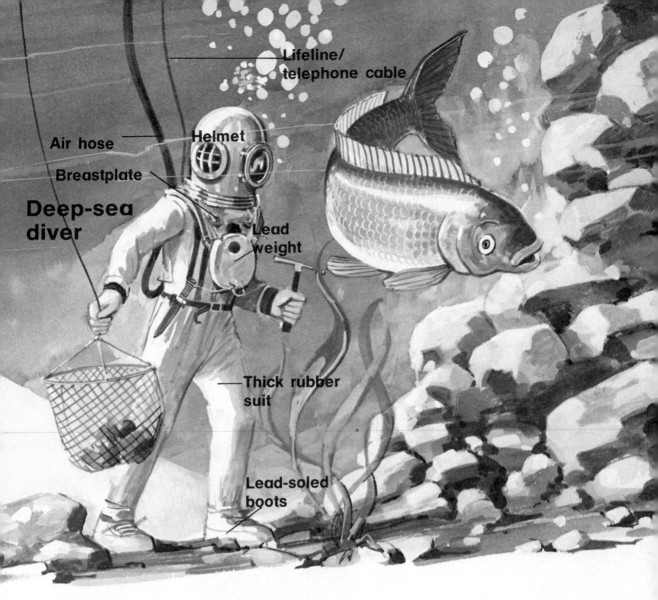

Lifeline/
telephone cable

Air hose

Helmet

Breastplate

**Deep-sea
diver**

Lead
weight

Thick rubber
suit

Lead-soled
boots

a protective suit. This is lined with foam insulation to keep his body warm.

Working divers often descend to their place of work in a diving bell. This was originally an open-ended vessel shaped like a bell. When it was lowered into the water, an air pocket was trapped inside, allowing people to work inside for a while. The modern diving bell is a chamber that can be pressurized and shut off from the water.

Much more cumbersome than scuba equipment is the helmet equipment worn by deep-sea divers. This is sup-plied with air from an airpump on a vessel on the surface. The air gives the diver oxygen and inflates his suit, which helps to counter the pressure of the water at great depths.

The diving suit is made of rubberized canvas and has a metal breastplate, to which the copper helmet is clamped. The helmet carries a telephone trans-mitter and receiver so that the diver can communicate with those on the surface. To keep him on the seabed the diver wears lead weights on his chest, a lead belt and lead boots.

Saturn

Astronaut

Moon

Into Space

We live today in one of the most exciting ages there has ever been. We have all kinds of novel machines and gadgets that make life easier and better. In particular we have machines that can whisk us speedily to anywhere on Earth, and even beyond Earth – into space.

To get into space we must be boosted away from Earth at an enormous speed, otherwise gravity will pull us back. The engine we use is the rocket. The space rocket works in much the same way as a fireworks rocket, only it is very much more powerful.

The vehicle we travel in is called a spacecraft. Most spacecraft that go into space, however, are not manned, but simply carry instruments and cameras. Those that stay close to Earth are called satellites. Those that fly deep into space to visit the planets, for example, are known as space probes.

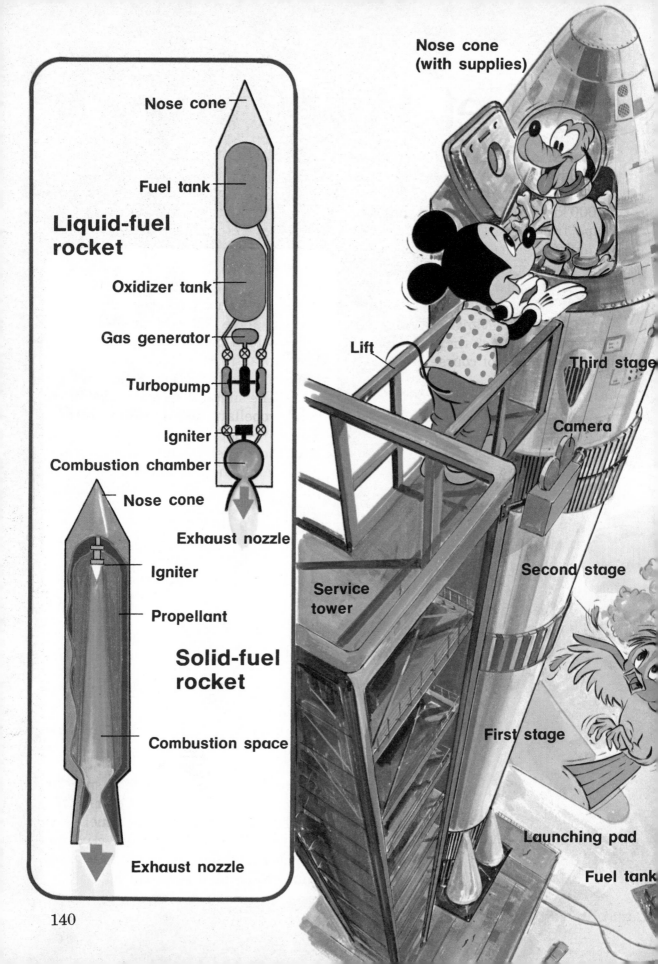

Liquid-fuel rocket

Nose cone

Fuel tank

Oxidizer tank

Gas generator

Turbopump

Igniter

Combustion chamber

Exhaust nozzle

Nose cone

Igniter

Propellant

Solid-fuel rocket

Combustion space

Exhaust nozzle

Nose cone (with supplies)

Lift

Third stage

Camera

Second stage

Service tower

First stage

Launching pad

Fuel tank

140

Rocket Power

To launch any object into space you must launch it from Earth at an enormous speed – at least 17,500 mph (28,000 km/h)! Only then can the object escape from Earth's pull, or gravity. The only engine that can make anything travel that fast is the rocket.

The rocket is also the only engine that can work in space. Other engines, like gasoline and jet engines, burn their fuel in oxygen which they suck in from the air. In space, of course, there is no air. The rocket works in space because it carries not only fuel, but also the oxygen with which to burn the fuel.

Rockets work much like jet engines. They burn fuel in a combustion chamber to make hot gases. The hot gases escape backward from a nozzle at an enormous speed. The force of these gases escaping backward creates a similar force forward (called 'reaction'), which propels the rocket.

In rocketry the fuel and oxygen-provider (oxidizer) are called propellants. The simplest kind of rocket has a solid propellant, like a firework rocket. The solid-fuel rocket consists really of only the rocket casing containing the propellant. There is a hole through the middle of the propellant which lets it burn from the middle outward rather than just from the end.

The most powerful space rockets, however, have liquid propellants and are much more complicated. Two common liquid fuels are kerosene and liquid hydrogen. Liquid hydrogen is hydrogen gas that has been cooled so much that it changes into liquid (just as steam changes into water when it is cooled). The most common oxidizer is liquid oxygen.

In a liquid rocket the propellants are pumped from their storage tanks into the combustion chamber. The pump is driven by a turbine, which is spun by gas produced in a gas generator. In the combustion chamber the fuel and oxidizer form an explosive mixture, which burns fiercely to produce gases that escape as a powerful jet.

Tracking antenna

Control building

Step by Step

To travel fast, space rockets need to burn several tons of propellants every minute, so they must carry thousands

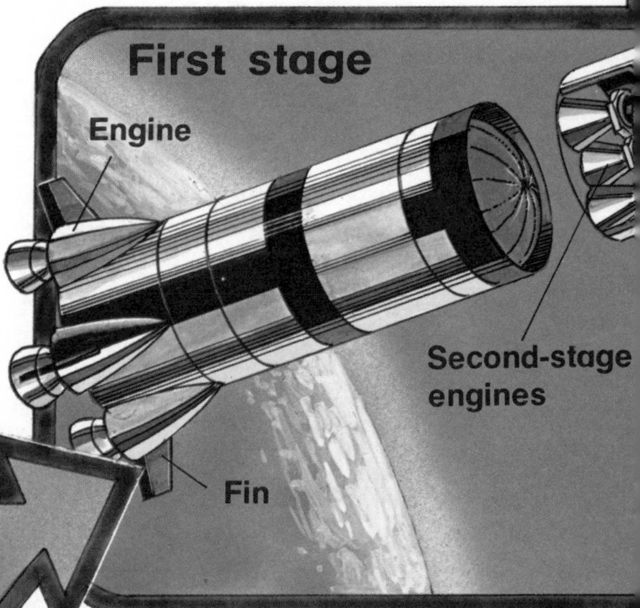

First stage

Engine

Second-stage engines

Fin

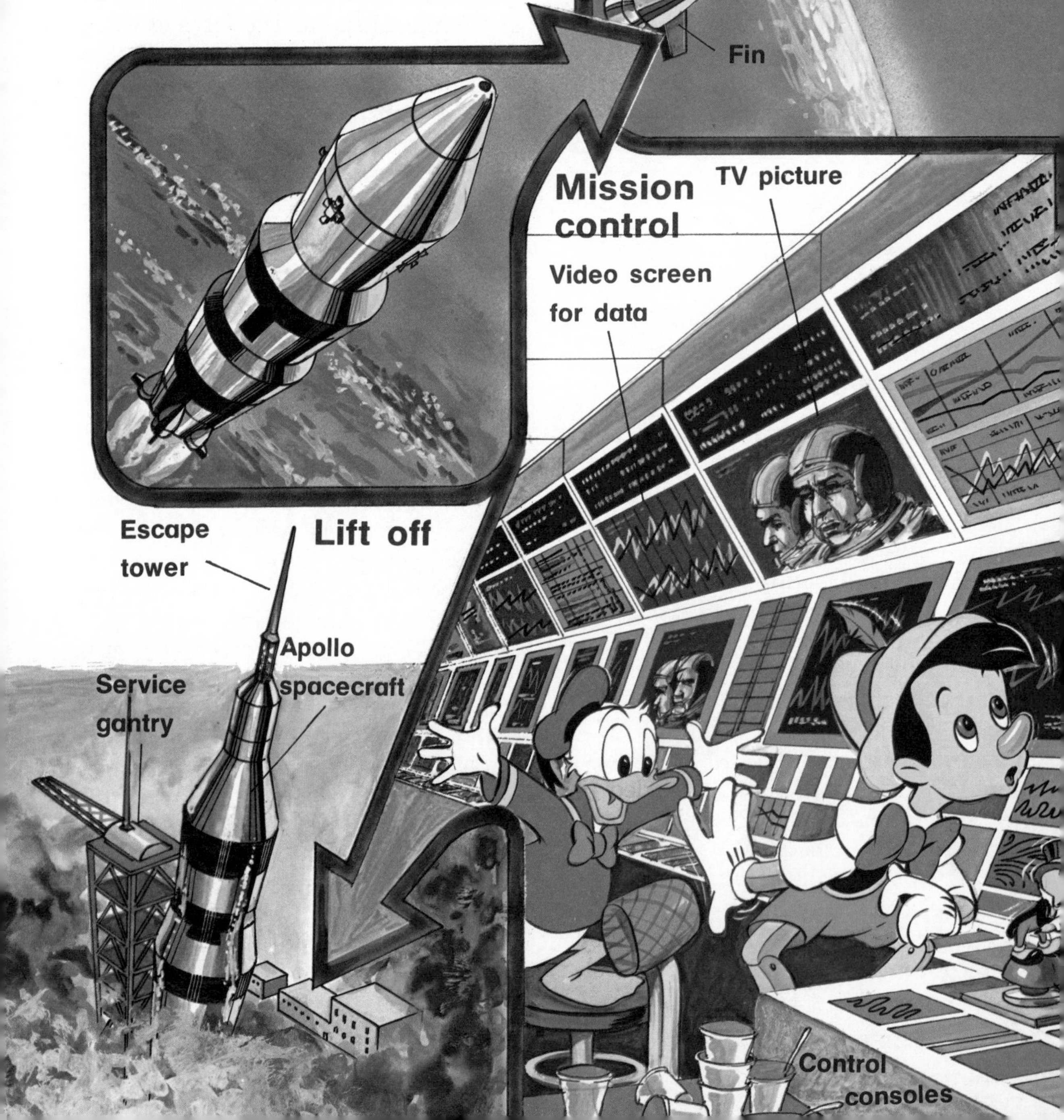

Mission control

TV picture

Video screen for data

Escape tower

Lift off

Apollo spacecraft

Service gantry

Control consoles

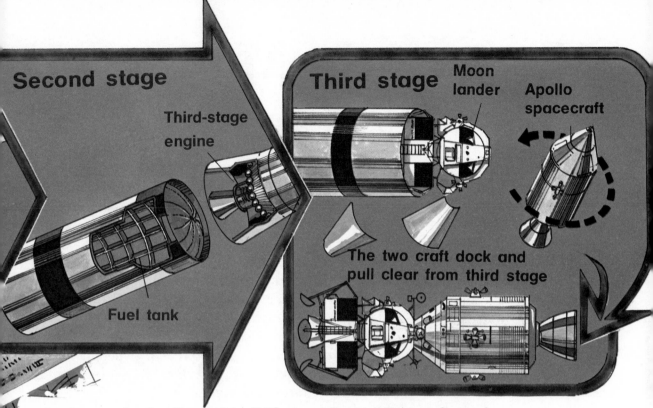

Second stage

Third-stage engine

Fuel tank

Third stage

Moon lander

Apollo spacecraft

The two craft dock and pull clear from third stage

upon thousands of gallons of fuel! That is why they are so big. Even so, however big it is, one rocket by itself cannot produce enough power to get into space.

The only way to get into space is to put several rockets on top of one another. The lower ones give the upper ones a "piggyback" ride into space. A space rocket built in this way is called a step-rocket. Each separate rocket is called a stage. Usually there are three stages and the rocket is called a three-stage launch vehicle.

The pictures show the most famous of all launch vehicles – the Saturn V moon rocket. On the launch pad it stood no less than 365 ft (111 meters) high! The astronauts were carried in the Apollo spacecraft in the nose of the rocket. Above them was an escape tower, which could lift them clear of the rocket if anything went wrong during launching. All the time they were in contact with the flight control-

lers at Mission Control.

Let us follow the Saturn V rocket into space. The flight director at Mission Control presses the firing button that ignites the rocket engines of the first (bottom) stage. Seconds later the huge rocket lifts off in sheets of flame and clouds of smoke.

After a few minutes, the first stage runs out of fuel, and falls away. The rockets of the second stage then fire and boost what remains of the vehicle faster and faster. Then the second stage runs out of fuel and in turn falls away. By this time the vehicle is traveling at over 15,000 mph (24,000 km/h) and is over 110 miles (180 km) above Earth. Finally, the third-stage rocket fires and boosts the vehicle into orbit around Earth.

Later, the third stage fires again to send the Apollo spacecraft toward the moon. Then the astronauts dock (link) the two parts of their craft together for the journey to the moon (page 148).

Firing button

Man-made Moons

Most of the craft that are sent into space do not have human crews. They are unmanned. Most of them are launched into orbit. In orbit they circle over the earth, traveling constantly in the same path. They always keep the same speed, too, because there is no air resistance to slow them down.

We call orbiting spacecraft "artificial satellites," or simply "satellites." We can also call them artificial moons, because in astronomy "satellite" is another word for a moon.

The first satellite was called Sputnik 1. It was sent into orbit by the Russians on October 4, 1957. Since then thousands of satellites have been launched. The most useful satellites have proved to be communications and weather satellites. A communications satellite relays (passes on) radio, telephone and television signals between continents.

One ground station (in, say, the United States) transmits signals to the communications satellite from a large aerial (antenna). The satellite receives the signals and amplifies (strengthens) them. Then it beams them down to another ground station (in, say, Britain). Many communications satellites are in high 22,300 miles (36,000 km) orbit on the equator above the Atlantic, Pacific and Indian Oceans. They include powerful Intelsat IV and V satellites. From these sites they can cover most of the world.

Most weather satellites orbit much lower, and travel over the poles. They can "see" more of the earth's surface as the earth spins beneath them. Weather satellites carry cameras and several instruments which record all kinds of data (information) about the earth's atmosphere and oceans and about the heat coming from the sun. The cameras take pictures which show the pattern of clouds covering the earth.

From the cloud pictures and other data taken day after day, weather forecasters are able to tell more accurately how the weather works. They can also issue warnings to ships, farmers and ordinary people when they see storms and hurricanes approaching.

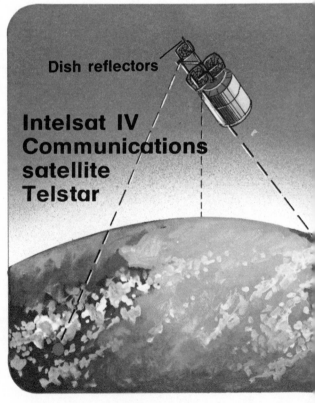

Dish reflectors

Intelsat IV Communications satellite Telstar

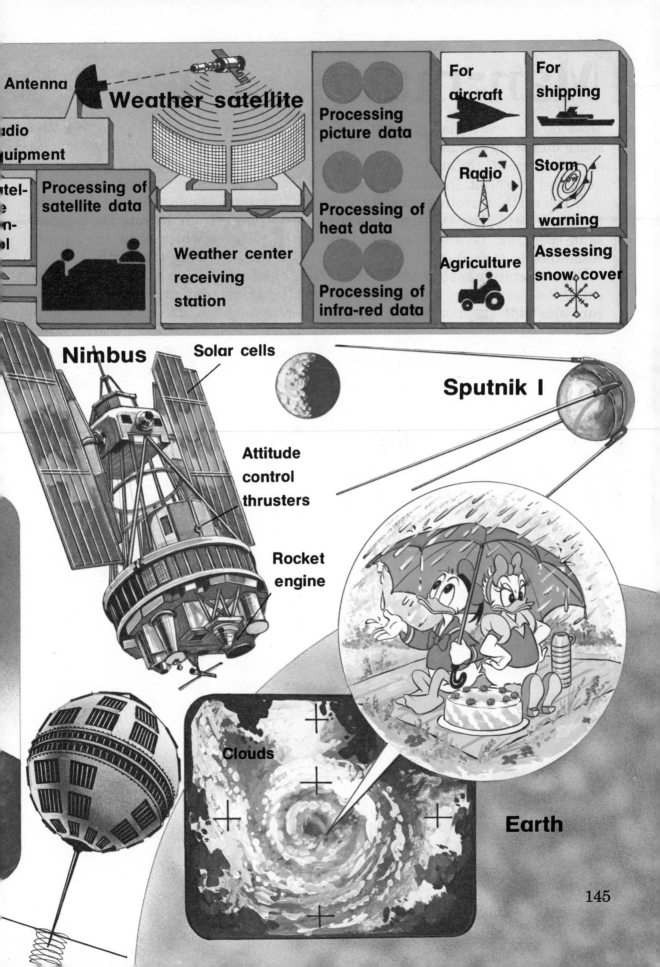

Antenna

Radio equipment

Satel-
lite
panel

Weather satellite

Processing of satellite data

Weather center receiving station

Processing picture data

Processing of heat data

Processing of infra-red data

For aircraft

For shipping

Radio

Storm warning

Agriculture

Assessing snow cover

Nimbus

Solar cells

Attitude control thrusters

Rocket engine

Sputnik I

Clouds

Earth

145

Empty fuel tank

4 Into orbit

Cargo bay

3 Jettison fuel tank

Main engines stop firing

Parachute compartment

Two smaller engines fire to put orbiter into orbit

2 Jettison boosters

Boosters away

External fuel tank

Shuttling into Space

On the average, about a hundred space launchings are made every year, mainly by the United States and Russia. The trouble with ordinary launching rockets is that they can be used only once. They disappear into the sky, never to return.

A new space launcher is now coming into use. It is the space shuttle. It is so called because it can shuttle (travel back and forth) into space. Most of it can be used again and again, so space launchings will become much cheaper.

The main part of the shuttle is the orbiter, which carries the crew and the payload (cargo). It is a cross between a plane and a spacecraft. It has the wings of a plane, but also the rocket engines of a spacecraft. It is about the size of a medium-sized airliner, being some 122 ft (37 meters) long with a wing-span of nearly 78 ft (24 meters).

Main engines continue firing

Orbiter

Main engines fire

1 Launch

Solid rocket boosters fire

5 Re-entry

Flight deck

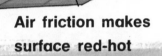

Air friction makes surface red-hot

The orbiter rides "piggyback" into space on top of a huge tank, which carries the fuel for its three main engines. On the launch pad, orbiter and fuel tank stand vertically. To the side of the fuel tank are strapped two rocket boosters. At launch (1) these boosters fire together with the orbiter's engines to thrust it into the heavens.

After a few minutes the boosters run out of fuel and separate (2). They then parachute back to Earth to be used again. Later the main fuel tank (3) empties and falls away. Two smaller engines then thrust the orbiter into orbit (4). After the mission is over the orbiter re-enters the atmosphere and is slowed down (5). Finally the orbiter glides to a runway landing (6).

6 Landing

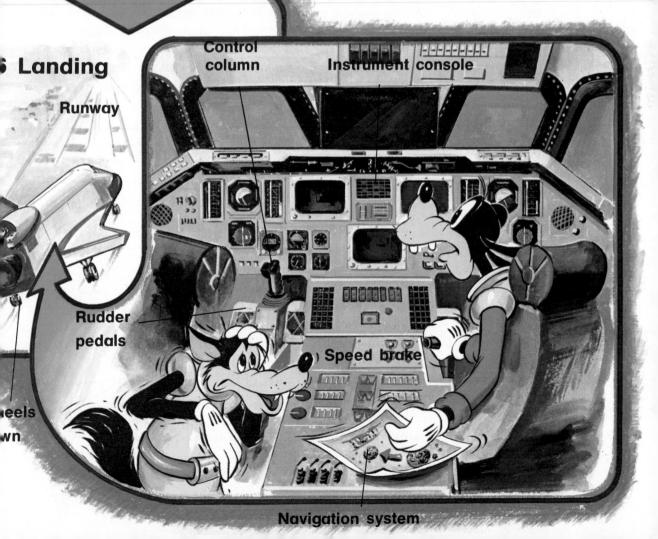

Runway

Control column

Instrument console

Rudder pedals

Speed brake

Wheels down

Navigation system

1 Saturn third stage fires

2 Docking operations

Earth

Third stage

Command and service module (CSM

Lunar module (LM)

We saw on pages 142-3 how the giant Saturn V rocket launched the Apollo spacecraft into space. Let us continue the story to see how the astronauts reach the moon.

In (1) we see the third stage of the rocket fire again to speed the astronauts toward the moon. Afterward the crew has to carry out a tricky docking operation (2) to get the craft into the right arrangement for the lunar (moon) landing. They separate the command and service module (CSM) from the third stage and then turn around and dock (link up) with the lunar module (LM), which puts them in

the position shown in (3). The Apollo spacecraft thus consists of three parts. The LM is the part that will actually land on the moon. The command module houses the crew, and the service module carries the main rocket engines, fuel and other equipment.

Eventually, after about three days, the Apollo spacecraft goes into orbit around the moon. Part of the crew goes into the LM, which then separates and descends to the moon (4).

After the LM has landed, the astronauts inside put on their spacesuits and go out to explore the surface of the moon (see pages 150-1). When they have finished, they climb back into the LM and prepare to rejoin the CSM, which has remained in orbit above them. They blast off in the upper part of the LM, called the ascent stage. They use the lower part, the descent stage, as a launch pad.

They time their lift off so that they meet up with the CSM while it is

148

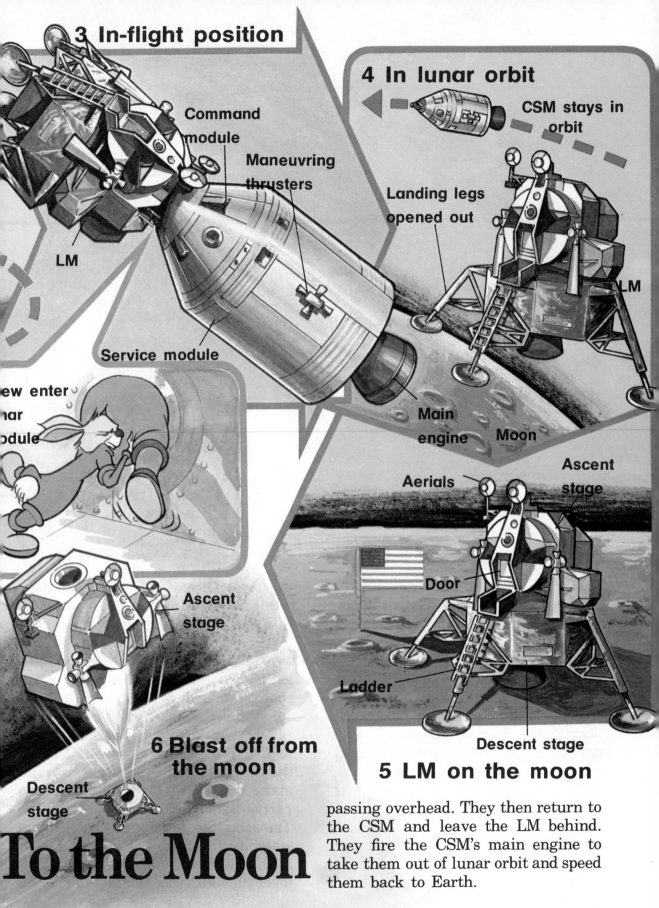

3 In-flight position

Command module

Maneuvring thrusters

LM

Service module

4 In lunar orbit

CSM stays in orbit

Landing legs opened out

LM

Main engine

Moon

ew enter
nar
odule

Ascent stage

Aerials

Ascent stage

Door

Ladder

Descent stage

5 LM on the moon

6 Blast off from the moon

Descent stage

To the Moon

passing overhead. They then return to the CSM and leave the LM behind. They fire the CSM's main engine to take them out of lunar orbit and speed them back to Earth.

149

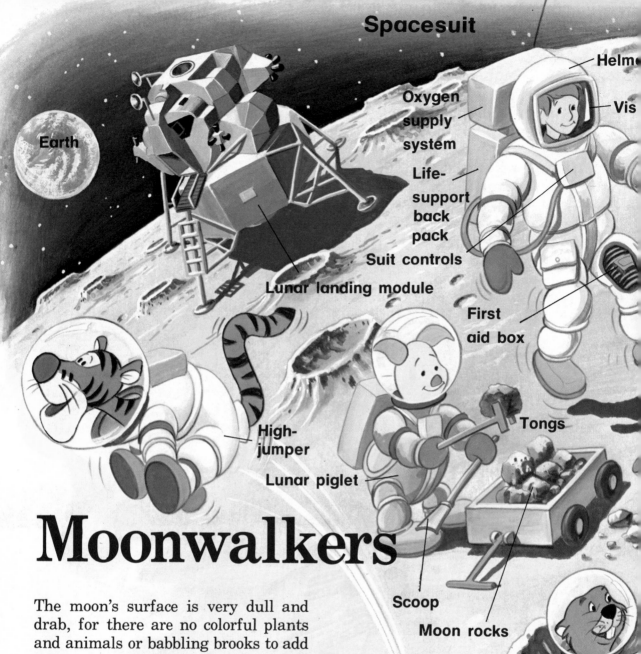

Helm[e]

Oxygen supply system

Vis[or]

Earth

Life-support back pack

Suit controls

Lunar landing module

First aid box

High-jumper

Tongs

Lunar piglet

Scoop

Moon rocks

Moonwalkers

The moon's surface is very dull and drab, for there are no colorful plants and animals or babbling brooks to add color and interest. There can be no plant and animal life because the moon has no atmosphere and no water. It is a totally dead world. Scientists and astronomers find the moon a fascinating place, for it is a different world. Knowing what the moon is like helps them to understand more about the rest of space.

The astronauts who explore the moon are kept very busy. They take samples of the soil on the moon and pick up moon rocks. They drill deep into the surface so that scientists back on Earth can look at the various layers underneath. This tells them about the moon's history. The astronauts also carry out scientific experiments and set up scientific stations which will work long after they return to Earth.

The moonwalkers must, of course, wear spacesuits on the moon. This gives them oxygen to breathe and also protects them from the heat and other rays from the sun. A spacesuit is made up of several layers. The layer next to the astronaut's skin is cooled by water, to prevent him getting too hot inside the suit. Over his head he has a transparent helmet and over the front of this, a gold-tinted visor. This protects his eyes from the fierce glare of the sun.

The astronauts travel in the lunar roving vehicle, better known as a moon buggy. The buggy is powered by electric motors on each wheel. The tires are made of woven piano wire. Its top speed is about 10 mph (16 km/h). It carries a TV camera and antenna and can relay pictures directly back to Earth.

The astronaut's backpack, which contains the oxygen, cooling water supply, radio and so on, looks very heavy. On Earth it is heavy, but on the moon it is very much lighter. This is because the moon's gravity is much less than the earth's – it is only one-sixth as strong. So a high jumper on the moon should be able to clear up to 40 ft (12 meters)! The low gravity makes ordinary walking quite difficult, and it is often better to hop rather than walk.

Dish aerial (antenna)

Instrument console

Aerial

Attitude indicator

Tool carrier

Sample stowage bays

Moon buggy

Crater

nera

TV camera

Wire tires

Commander

Magnetic boots

Space Stations

The space shuttle (pages 146-7) now coming into use can carry an enormous load into space – up to 30 tons. It can carry cargo as long as 60 ft (18 meters) and 15 ft (4½ meters) in diameter. For several years it will be used mainly to launch satellites and to fly a space laboratory called Spacelab into orbit.

In the future, however, it will be used to ferry parts to build a space station. The various parts will be put together in orbit to make a large craft in which dozens of people will be able to live and work for months at a time. They will be scientists, engineers and doctors who will carry out all kinds of experiments.

Eventually huge space stations will be built hundreds of meters across. One is shown in the picture. It looks a very odd shape, but this does not matter in space. It does not have to be streamlined like a plane, because there is no air in space.

The living quarters of the space station may be rotated to produce an artificial gravity. The rotation produces a force (centrifugal force) pressing things against the walls of the vessel. This imitates gravity. Other parts of the station will be stationary. People working in them will be weightless. To keep their feet firmly on the floor (or on the ceiling for that matter!) they will need to wear magnetic boots.

A spacecraft like this could one day be fitted out as an interplanetary cruise ship, able to travel the thousands upon thousands of miles between one planet and another. It would be fitted with powerful nuclear engines. It would have a farming area to provide the crew with fresh food. The crew would live mainly on plants raised in large domed greenhouse modules, but they might also farm quick-growing fish in artificial ponds.

Control center

Electronic instrument bays

Index

Acknowledgements

We would like to express our thanks to everyone who helped in the production of this book, and in particular the following people:

Picture research by Gael Hayter.
Information and reference material provided by: Auto Wrappers (Norwich) Ltd. 92-3; Brick Development Association 100-1; British Hovercraft Corporation 122-3; Building Centre 100-1; Carpet Manufacturers Federation 14-15; Cement and Concrete Association 100-1; Coca Cola Ltd. 90-1; Crossley and Sons Ltd. 100-1; Courtaulds Ltd. 18-19; Daily Telegraph 86-7; Danepak Ltd. 92-3; Elton Packaging Systems Ltd. 92-3; Forgrove Machinery Ltd. (Leeds) 92-3; Glass Manufacturers Federation 102-3; Halls Barton Ropery Co. Ltd. 14-15; HJ Heinz Co. Ltd. 90-1; ICI Fibres Ltd. 18-19; Metromethods Ltd. 92-3; Ministry of Defence (Royal Navy) 134-5; Pilkington Brothers Ltd. 102-3; Reed Group Ltd. 78-82; Rowntree Mackintosh 92-3; Stal Laval Ltd. 130-1; United Glass Ltd. 102-3; Vickers Oceanics 136-7; John Watney Photographic Agency 80-1, 106-7, 132-3; Josiah Wedgwood and Sons Ltd. 96-7; White Fish Authority 118-19; Wiggins Teape Ltd. 78-82; Windsor and Newton Ltd. 56-7.